The Obedient Child

Joyce Marleau

STELLAR
COMMUNICATIONS
HOUSTON

Houston, Texas

THE OBEDIENT CHILD
Copyright © 2021 by Joyce Marleau
Published by Stellar Communications Houston

This book is protected under the copyright laws of the United States of America. Any reproduction or other unauthorized use of the material herein is prohibited without the express written permission of the author.

For information, contact Stellar Communications Houston at www.stellarwriter.com.

The author has endeavored to recreate events, locales, and conversations with accuracy.

Hardcover ISBN: 978-1-944952-36-5
Library of Congress Control Number: 2020924014

Stellar Communications Houston
www.stellarwriter.com
281-804-7089

I want to dedicate this book to honor my parents. I have an enormous sense of gratitude and appreciation to them for giving so much of themselves. I regret that I never thanked them before their passing.

CONTENTS

Acknowledgments	ix
Preface	xi
Introduction	xiv
Japan: Part I	1
"Obedient Child"	11
Less Than Perfect Wasn't Good Enough	17
The Third Red Stripe	18
Good Citizens, Respectable Families	19
Japan: Part II	22
The Shock of War	23
Escaping to Lukang	28
The War Comes to Lukang	30
Surviving the War	32
China	39
Taipei	39
Second Girls' Middle School	40
Testing Boundaries	45
Walking the Middle Road	49
Leaving Home	53
America: Part I	55
Dorm Life	58
Religion	59
Back to the Sea	61
Seattle	62
"Do You Intend to Marry Me Or Not?"	67

America: Part II — 71
- *Meanwhile – Back in Taiwan* — 80
- *Starting to Invest in Real Estate* — 82
- *Boeing Layoff* — 85
- *Teenagers* — 91
- *Ama and Akon* — 94

Around the World — 98
- *Japan* — 98
- *Taiwan* — 103
- *The United States* — 104
- *The Philippines* — 106
- *China* — 110

Mexico — 116
- *Miramar House (Casa el Balcon)* — 127
- *Second Construction – House on Iturbide Street* — 135
- *Enjoying Spending Time in Mexico* — 139

The Middle of the Road — 140

Postscript — 150

ACKNOWLEDGMENTS

I WOULD FIRST LIKE TO THANK THE MOST IMPORTANT PERSON who helped me on my book, my husband, Joseph Marleau, who spent a lot of time verifying old family information, offering to use some of his suggestions, helping with some editing, and being there to answer questions.

I would also like to thank the following people who helped me in verifying and providing the information for my book:

My cousin, Ting Shou Zhen丁守真, who went to Fujian, China, to visit many Ting relatives for the first time after the Second World War when China reclaimed Taiwan from Japan. He became one of the three honorable presidents of the Chen Dai Publication Committee of Ting Hui Clan Genealogy 陳埭丁氏回族宗譜. He brought many copies of the book to distribute to relatives in Taiwan, which is how I found out about the incredible, documented Ting ancestral family history and is what motivated me to take my two teenage grandchildren to visit the Ting ancestral temples and tombs and meet some distant relatives.

My younger sister, Eileen Wu. She helped me in verifying the details of ancestral documents and provided her own achievement at the university and her teaching career (*Japan One* and *America One* and *Around the World*).

My second cousin, Dora Shu-fang Dien. She verified the Ting ancestral documents (*Japan One*) and provided a copy of her biography. In addition, she gave her permission to mention her book, which has the Ting ancestral history and Taiwan, etc.

My first younger brother, Yih-Long Ting or Lee. He gave me permission to write about his challenging teenage experience and verified his university education and career experience.

My second younger brother, Elon Ting. I verified with him his university education and career experience, as well as details about taking care of the parents.

My daughter, Karen Coe, who verified her difficult teenage period both at the school and at home and gave me the achievements of her high school and university education as a pharmacist and dentist. She also verified how she met her husband.

My daughter, Linda Marleau, who gave me the information of her achievements during the time she was employed as an engineer designer of the City of Seattle.

Finally, I would like to thank Jennifer Rizzo and Dana Robinson of The Writers for Hire, Inc., who did an excellent job of reviewing and editing my very detailed life stories from different cultures to finalize my biography. It was a lot of work for me but was an enjoyable experience. Also, Ella Ritchie of Stellar Communications Houston for helping me to go through the publication of the book. I was able to stay through the whole process because I had the encouragement from both Jenni and Ella.

PREFACE

IN MAY OF 1980, I WAS WORKING IN THE KITCHEN WHEN THE phone rang. It was a cousin, whom I hardly was in contact with, calling from Taiwan to inform me that a classmate from my Japanese grade school was wishing to re-connect with me. I attended that school when I lived in Keelung, Taiwan, in the late 1930s, during the Japanese occupation so long ago.

She was calling me after all this time to find out what happened to me, her best friend. She also wanted to tell me that our classmates had been having reunions in Japan for many years and wanted to invite me to come. She had seen my cousin's name in one of their alumni books, recognized the last name, and thought he must be my older brother, so she contacted him looking for me. He gave me her phone number in Japan and said that I should give her a call.

This was such a stunning revelation from so long ago. I was very concerned that I wouldn't even be able to converse in Japanese. I had not spoken nor heard much of the language in about 40 years, having been totally immersed in two completely different cultures, learning Chinese and English.

For several days I had those thoughts, but I finally determined that I would call her and apologize for my broken Japanese. And so I dialed the number. Immediately upon hearing her voice, the Japanese came out of my mouth almost as good as when we were together in grade school. It is amazing that the sound of a familiar voice can stimulate the memory in such a fantastic way. It was an indescribable feeling that I was able to reclaim my Japanese culture. All the memories of that period started to surge to my mind.

My father, who was faithful in preserving documents, had given me some books and documents on his earliest ancestors who came from Persia to China, dating from 1260. He also gave me a book on the first family members to immigrate to Taiwan in 1812, which contains the family trees of the generations from 1812 to the 23rd generation, which is my generation.

In reading those documents and the book, I was amazed at how much work was involved in writing both history books with many names of ancestors from so many years ago. I realized that the Chinese culture really values keeping a family history.

During my generation, after the Second World War, the western world was open to many Asian countries. There was a shortage of schools in Taiwan because of the arrival of many Chinese from the Mainland. The Government started to allow high school graduates and university students to study abroad. The first requirement was that you had to apply and receive the scholarship. English was a required course in the middle schools. A lot of young students started to apply to study in other countries, especially in the U.S. There were some expenses you had to pay, the airfare, and the security deposit of $2,000 USD. It was very expensive for us but my siblings and I, one by one after graduating high school, left for the U.S. to study. My father was able to sell a piece of inherited land to cover those costs. I shall always be so grateful to him for doing that for me. Both of my parents were educators and they knew how important education was.

After I came to the U.S. and attended college in 1952, my life changed dramatically. In 1957, when I was 24 years old, I married an American. My life was so Americanized that we only spoke English in our house. During that period, the world was not so global as today.

The thing that I regretted most is that I never attempted to teach my daughters Chinese or Japanese. After many years, many young students who were studying abroad were scattered to many parts of the world and gradually got disconnected. I have been in the U.S. for close to 70 years, but as far as I know, there is no one in charge of writing the third family book for my generation.

When my grandchildren were in their teens, I took them to visit the Ting ancestral temples and the houses in China and Taiwan. I wanted to show them the places and have them meet some of the distant relatives, so they have some idea of the Ting ancestors.

Joe and I started to travel more and interact with many people from different cultures. Especially as I get older, many friends and the people whom we meet are younger. Quite often, whenever I tell them the things which happened in my life or the experiences I had, unequivocally, most of them say that I should write a book, and they would like to have a copy when the book is finished.

When I started to approach my late 80s and began to reflect more on my life, I felt strongly that I truly have had an exceptional life, and that it is very important for me to pass my ancestral history to my family and descendants. All my family members only speak English and those documents and books are mostly written in Chinese. With this in mind, I have decided to at least write my autobiography.

Joyce Morleau

INTRODUCTION

It was hot and humid that morning on the train. Hotter than I was used to. I had forgotten how hot Japan can be in the summer. But then again, it could have just been nerves. It had been so long since I had seen any of these people, over 40 years! How would they feel about me after all this time? What would we have to talk about? Would I even still be able to remember the language?

The train stopped in front of a large department store. This was my stop. I knew if I cut through the basement, then ran upstairs to the main street, that I would be able to save myself some time and get to the meeting place quickly. I did not want to be late.

The basement was full of bolts of fabric, and I was weaving in and out of them, making pretty good time, when all of a sudden something stopped me in my tracks. I had caught the tiniest whiff of a smell, something familiar. I reached over and grabbed one of the bolts of fabric. It was an inexpensive roll of dyed cloth, but the smell was so strong; that dye, that chemical, so familiar, but I just couldn't place it. I leaned my head against a nearby pillar, closed my eyes, and reached back into my memory.

As I stood there with my eyes closed, holding the fabric up to my nose, a wave of emotions swept over me. I finally recalled what it was. This was the smell of my mother. This fabric, used to make everyday common kimonos worn by Japanese women, was also worn by my mother every time she took me shopping, when we went on outings, and when we met up with her friends who also wore these informal kimonos and smelled like this. I had to hold on to the pillar for balance, as all of the memories came flooding back to my mind.

Our house was the only one made of brick on our street. All of the others were made of wood, which was more typical in Taiwan in the 1930s. Our parents had created a play area in part of the front yard for me and my four siblings to play. It had a sandbox, a swing, and a pull-up bar, but my favorite thing to do was climb the huge Gajumaru, Banyan, and Ficus trees in our garden. I created my own world inside those trees. Some of their trunks were so big I could lie down in them and play house all by myself.

Our front garden was pretty big, and it became sort of a playground for our friends from school and the other children in the neighborhood. My friend, Tohara Shigeko, came over to play a lot, and we liked to build sandcastles and hide special sticks or stones inside them, or try to destroy each other's castle by throwing more sand on them.

When I heard my mother's voice calling, "Jun chan," I knew that our playtime was over. I knew she would soon come outside, close the gate behind our friends, and escort me back inside the house. It was time for me to study, practice my calligraphy, or go to dance class.

JAPAN

Part I

TO UNDERSTAND MY LIFE, it's important to first understand where I come from and who my ancestors are. This is not a simple thing to explain. Some people can say, "I'm Chinese," or "I came from Taiwan," and so on. But my story is a little more complicated than that.

My father's name was Ting Ruey-Yang 丁瑞鍈. "Ting" was his family name. In most Asian cultures, the family name goes before the given name, and my father was very proud of his ancestry. The Tings were a family of prominent merchants who came to China from Persia sometime between 1265 and 1274 during the Silk Road trade. According to our family genealogy, the first generation who settled in Quanzho 廣州, China, was a Muslim merchant called Ting Jin 丁謹 (1251-1298). He was said to have been the second grandson of Sayyid Ejell Sham Al-Din, who was a 31st generation descendant of the prophet Mohammed. I have a close family member, Dora Shu-Fang Dien 丁淑芳, who was a Professor Emeritus of Human Development at California State University and attended a lot of lectures on the Silk Road and the Sogdians, an ancient Iranian civilization that played an important role in the silk trade. Dora's book, called

Growing Up in Three Cultures: A Personal Journey of a Taiwanese-American Woman, includes a comprehensive family ancestral history in the first and second chapters. She wrote to us that our possible ancestor, the son of the king of Bukhara, who followed Genghis Kahn to China, was a Sogdian. If that is the case, then our ancestors were not Arabs.

In either case, the pedigree of the Ting family settled in Quanzhou to do business during 1265-1274. As the men married local women, and the families began to grow and prosper, some of them eventually moved to Fujian 福建 and the nearby provinces. Others simply crossed the strait and settled in Taiwan.

The first Ting ancestor, Ting Teng-Ju 丁樸實, who was my great great great grandfather, came to Taiwan in about 1812, but the Ting ancestral temple is still in Fujian, China. Several years ago, I took my two grandchildren there to visit it. There are both a mosque and a temple on the property as evidence of the family's gradual conversion from Islam to Buddhism, from Persian to Chinese. On the tombs inside the Muslim cemetery are the names of the male members of the family written in Arabic. On the wall of the temple are listed the 14 Imperial scholars from the Ting family, a title given only to those highly educated men who served the Chinese Imperial court. Ting Shou-Quan 丁壽泉, my great grandfather, is the last name on the list in 1884.

My father was born in the Fujian Province, but when he was just a young boy, his immediate family joined their Ting relatives in Lukang 鹿港, Taiwan 臺灣. Lukang was a prosperous port city, and the Tings there built a large complex where all the male heirs could live with their families.

My father was the youngest of five children, and his father died before he was born. Women at that time were limited in their ability

> Taiwan has gone by many names during its long history with the most enduring, Formosa, dating back to the 16th century. Portuguese sailors were impressed by the island's beautiful scenery and dubbed the place "Ilha Formosa" or "Beautiful Island" on their maps.

First Generation, 1251–1298

Fourth Generation, 1243–1420

Eighth Generation, 1473–1522

Eleventh Generation, 1569–1636

Eighteenth Generation, 1800–1875

My paternal grandfather, who passed away before Father was born.

My paternal grandmother with bound feet.

to earn an income, so his mother had to rely on his older brothers and extended family to support them. Luckily for my father, the free government-run education system in Taiwan was excellent, so he was still able to get a very good education even though his family was poor. He just had to pass the examinations.

My father was a good student. Because of his hard work and diligence, he did well in both grade school and high school and was accepted to a prestigious university in Japan called Hitotsubashi University 一橋大学, where he studied business and economics. Hitotsubashi is still considered one of the top universities in the world for commerce-related subjects. Since his older brothers helped support him while he was in school, my father was able to dedicate himself to his studies, impress many of his professors, and graduate at the top of his class.

After he graduated, my father left Japan and returned to Taiwan. Almost immediately, one of my father's acquaintances who knew my maternal grandfather, Yen Guo-Nian 顏國年, offered to be a matchmaker for my father. He soon introduced my father to a young Taiwanese woman named Yen May 顏梅.

As you can probably guess, Yen May was my mother. Yen Guo-Nian was my maternal grandfather.

My parents only met two times before they got married. The first time, they were sitting down formally across a table, and my mother's head was bowed so low that she could barely lift her eyes above the buttons on my father's jacket to see his face. But somehow, that was enough.

Father as a university student.

I can understand why my father's professor thought he would be a good match for Yen May. They were both young and highly educated; like the rest of the Yen family, May was a scholar. She'd left home at age 11 to study in Japan.

They were also both descendants from prosperous families: My mother's ancestors came to Taiwan from Mainland China in 1775. Under the Japanese rule of Taiwan, Yen Xun-Fang 顏尋芳 my great grandfather, and his brother, Yen Zheng Chun 顏正春, established a large coal and gold mining enterprise in the Keelung area, and it quickly became very prosperous. Later, when my grandfather and his brother established the name for the mining company, they called it 臺陽礦業株式會社. By the time I was born, they had owned about 49 acres of property that was beautifully landscaped with large ponds, gazebos, and creeks. The green hills were dotted with mansions belonging to my grandfather, his brother, and a few of my mother's male cousins. The entrance was guarded with large iron gates, but the Yen family was very generous and allowed the public to come inside and enjoy the estate, much like a public park. In the very front, closest to the street, sat the office building for the Yen coal and gold mining company.

My maternal Grandfather. The medals on his chest were awarded for contributing many charitable efforts, including opening his estate as a public park.

Despite their similarities in education and background, my parents were also quite different. My mother was always interested in reading and writing literature. Those pursuits, along with taking care of us, limited the time she had to be concerned with her appearance. Once I became a teenager and started to pay more attention to how I looked, I noticed that she wore simple clothes and rarely did anything with

Mother's Yen Family members in Yen's Temple. I am standing in front of my Mother, third from left with Father and two brothers. This is a very special photo of Mother's family: There are 10 children (6 boys and 4 girls) in the family. Five younger brothers in school uniform are standing in the back. Seated from left are the first younger sister and her family, my family, Mother, the third younger sister, Father, the first younger brother and his family, and at the very right is the second younger sister.

her face. She might start to comb her hair, but then see an interesting article that she wanted to read, get distracted writing in her poetry book, or see that one of us children needed something, and she would completely forget about her hair.

My father was exactly the opposite. He was always well-dressed and well-groomed; he looked every bit the part of the successful businessman he was. He had gone to work for my grandfather in the mining company as soon as they were married and didn't squander the opportunity. He did very well right from the start.

After graduating from high school, my mother took the entrance exam to Ochanomizu Joshi Daigaku お茶の水女子大学, the most prestigious women's teaching university in Japan. Tuition for Ochanomizu was inexpensive, and students from any financial background could apply—but the university only accepted 1 out of every 10 applicants. The competition was very steep, but my mother was accepted. This was so exceptional that the local newspaper wrote an article about her.

Mother as a university student.

After she graduated from the university, my mother was offered a position teaching Japanese at a girls' high school in her hometown of Keelung, Taiwan.

This was quite incredible at the time: a Taiwanese woman, teaching the Japanese language to Japanese students who were living in Taiwan. Under the Japanese rule, even in our own country, the Taiwanese people were treated as inferior. The Qing Dynasty had ceded Taiwan to Japan in 1895 during the Treaty of Shimonoseki, which ended the First Sino-Japanese War, and Taiwan had been governed by Japanese colonial rule ever since.

My parents

This meant that Japanese people in Taiwan received the best education, were in positions of power, held the best jobs, and were the most prosperous and respected. Japanese was even considered the official language of Taiwan. Taiwanese people, on the other hand, especially those who did not speak Japanese, were considered lower-class citizens, went to inferior schools, and held lower-paying jobs.

Our family tried very hard to be a model of acceptable Taiwanese behavior. We lived our lives according to Japanese culture, with no discernable difference between us and the Japanese citizens living around us.

Our house had been a dowry gift from my maternal grandfather when my parents got married. It was a traditional, tatami-style Japanese duplex with large rooms and traditional straw mats on the floor. The outside was brick, and it was much larger than any of the others in our neighborhood. It had a nicely landscaped entrance, trees, plants, and a playground.

My parents' wedding. Grandfather is second from right in the front row. Grandmother is third from left in the front row.

On our front door hung an official plaque that read: *Japanese Language Family.* Directly behind our home were the small houses of the Taiwanese families, the uneducated laborers of the city, who spoke only Taiwanese.

I was not allowed to speak anything other than Japanese. Even when my mother's family came over to visit, who only spoke Taiwanese, I would smile and greet them in Japanese, and then I would sit quietly and listen to all of them talking, absorbing all of their language that I could, never daring to utter a word of it.

It was strange when these two worlds came together. It was always that way: Japan and Taiwan, the old and the new. Different languages and customs. Two worlds existing with my family somewhere in between.

My maternal grandmother, Sie Man, was not even educated. My grandfather, Yen Guo Nian, died very young, around age 51, and after that my grandmother lived with her oldest son, my uncle, Yen Tsan-Hai 顏滄海.

I remember her coming to visit us often. Her facial features were so elegant, and her feet partially bound. She was so beautiful to me. She often came with my aunts and they always walked, under the hot sun, carrying their umbrellas to protect their smooth Taiwanese skin. At some point she became a devout Buddhist and vegetarian.

Maternal Grandmother

Whenever she joined us for a meal, we had to be so careful not to contaminate her food. We used a separate bowl and separate utensils in the preparation, and as we sat around the table, we were not allowed to pass any serving dishes that might contain meat over her plate. We showed great respect for our grandmother.

"Obedient Child"

My mother always felt more at home in the Japanese culture than in either Chinese or Taiwanese. I'm sure this was due, at least in part, to the fact that she'd been educated in Japan. But I think there was another, more personal reason for this feeling.

When my mother first went to school in Japan, her parents were required to fill out a lot of lengthy paperwork for the admissions department, giving detailed information about all the members of her family. As she was reading through the paperwork before submitting it to the school, she noticed some very disturbing information about her father.

My mother was the oldest of 10 children, so she knew her family paperwork would be quite lengthy. When she went to turn it in, however, she noticed there were even more names listed than she expected to see. Quite a few more, in fact. Her parents had listed the names of six more children—children that my mother had never heard of, plus the name of her father's second wife: Lin Ji Shi 林寄市.

Not only was it surprising to find out her father had married a second wife and had six other children she had never met, but the custom of having a second wife was something Japanese people never did. It was a little more common among Chinese people, but not Japanese. Japanese men were known to sometimes take a mistress, but never a second wife.

My mother was shocked and ashamed, so much that she hardly spoke to her father for two years. Years later, when she married my father, she made one thing very clear. Even though she was otherwise perfectly submissive, she would not tolerate him having a second wife.

And he never did.

Despite her affinity for Japanese culture, my mother did follow some Chinese traditions, as well. For example, according to our ancestral Chinese tradition, my maternal grandfather, Yen Guo Nian, had the honor of giving me my name at birth. Although the written characters are the same in both Chinese and Japanese, 丁淳兒, the pronunciation is very different. In Chinese, my name is Chwen Erl, but in Japanese, it is Jun Ji. In either case, it means "obedient child."

That name definitely seemed to fit: I was the second-oldest of five children in our family, but I was the oldest daughter. As a Taiwanese educator of Japanese girls, my mother knew that how she raised her own daughter would be watched very closely. She also knew that education would be the key to my future.

Me as an infant, sitting on Father's lap. My older brother, Robert, is standing, and Mother is holding my younger brother, Lee.

My family during the Japanese occupation. From left: Mother, my youngest brother Elon Ting 丁逸郎, *myself* 丁淳兒, *younger sister* 丁玲兒, *older brother* 丁逸民; *younger brother* 丁逸龍; *and Father.*

All levels of the provincial schools in Taiwan were supported by the government, but students were required to pass an entrance exam to get in. The better the school, the more difficult the exam. If you failed the exam at one school, you had to take an exam at a lower school, and if you failed several times in a row, you were forced to go to a low-rated private school at your own cost. The highest-rated government schools had the highest number of applicants, and the entrance exams were more difficult. Graduates from those schools got the best jobs. Education really was the key to your future life, and that future began in kindergarten.

My mother began preparing me for the kindergarten oral entrance examination early. She taught me how to address elders, how to hand

One of my performances on stage.

I am dressed for the celebration of the Traditional Shichi Go San (7-5-3 Years old) Girls Festival Day. Shichi-go-san (Japanese for "Seven-Five-Three") is described by Britannica as "one of the most important festivals for Japanese children, observed annually on November 15. Girls of three and seven years of age and boys of five years of age are taken by the parents to the Shinto shrine of their tutelary deity to offer thanks for having reached their prospective age and to invoke blessing for the future." "Shinto" is a Japanese religion.

things to others, and the proper use of words. We had a big calendar on the wall, with lessons and classes marked on every day of the week.

Then, on Saturdays and Sundays, my mother would dress me in a beautiful formal kimono, sit me in the back of our elegant black Jinrikisha 人力車 (a human-powered vehicle), and send me to Japanese dance class. A tiny me, up so high and sitting straight up, hands folded in my lap. A perfect, obedient Japanese girl, just the way my mother trained me.

I couldn't help but feel sorry for the Jinrikisha man, sweating and running to get me to dance class on time, but I never said anything to him.

Our class often accepted invitations to perform for school events or for different organizations around the city. One time, we were invited to dance for a group of wounded soldiers, and when we got there, it turned out to be at the large Japanese-style event facility on my grandfather's estate. Yen Guo-Nian owned the gold and coal mine in the Keelung area and was a very wealthy man, but he was also very charitable. His Yen family was involved in many civic endeavors and his large estate in the center of town was often used for receptions for heads of state and formal occasions. This time he had opened up space for soldiers to convalesce, and I was there to perform.

That beautiful event facility, where the Japanese Imperial family members had once visited, was also offered for the wounded soldiers, dressed in the white gowns of the infirmed. The ashes of their fallen comrades were displayed high up on shelves around the room, as a sign of honor. This image has stayed with me my whole life.

Less Than Perfect Wasn't Good Enough

I started school when I was 5 years old. Our family was considered a National Language Family, which meant we spoke only Japanese in our house, and my siblings and I were eligible to attend the much higher-rated Japanese speaking schools in Taiwan.

I often felt as if I went to two schools every day, the Japanese school during the day, then the one at home with my mother at night.

Every day when I got home from school, my mother would watch over me while I did my homework, my own personal tutor. She made certain that my calligraphy was perfect. She made sure that everything was perfect.

And, her hard work paid off: When the teacher read aloud the names of the highest scores in the class, my name was always called. I remember being so excited to bring home my very first report card in the first grade. I came dancing and singing into the house, proudly holding the card with mostly As and two Bs. I even got a pencil as a prize!

I thought I had done pretty well, so I did not understand why my mother looked so sad. Without saying a word, she took the report card from my hands and sat in silence on the tatami for a very long time, while I danced around with my new pencil.

It wasn't until I was an adult, many years later, that I understood the pressure and the disappointment my mother must have felt that day. No matter how hard we tried to be like the Japanese people around us, we were Taiwanese and would always be discriminated against.

Anything less than straight As, anything less than perfect in every way, would never be good enough in their eyes.

The Third Red Stripe

My first report card might have been a disappointment, but I did make my mother proud as I progressed through school.

Japanese education was not only academic, it was also physical. Our school day began with exercises on the sports field, with the teacher standing on a platform demonstrating the routines as music played in the background.

In the summertime, we learned to swim. Japan is surrounded by water, so knowing how to swim is of the utmost importance to Japanese people. My mother had been giving me personal swimming lessons since I was 5, so by the time I got to school, I didn't have any problems.

One girl in my class was afraid of the waves and didn't want to go in. The teacher picked her up and threw her right into the ocean. Not with gentle coercion, but by force, which was the typical Japanese way of educating.

By the time I was 9 years old, I was quite an accomplished swimmer. As a test of endurance, upon completion of our lessons, they took us to the deeper part of the ocean and made us parallel to the shore for 500 meters. There were so many people, and we had to stay in a perfect line. We had to dodge being kicked and make our own little spot in the water.

When we made it back to land, they gave us a red stripe to put on our black swimsuits, as a sign of our accomplishment. After that, I swam the 1000-meter endurance test, twice as far as the first one, and I got a second red stripe to put on my swimsuit.

But the final test was the toughest by far, 3000 meters. I was so nervous, but my mother assured me that I could do it. We swam way out, a lot deeper in the ocean than before, and swam parallel to the shore. The water was so choppy, and the salt stung my throat and eyes.

The shore looked so far away, and I felt so small. I just tucked my head down and started swimming, and by the time I made it all the way back to the shore, my legs were covered in seaweed.

The first thing I did was look for my mother's face.

When I found her, I could see that she was elated. She was so proud of me when I received that third red stripe.

Good Citizens, Respectable Families

School in Japan was very different from the way school is here in the U.S. Teachers were some of the most respected people in the community and they took their jobs very seriously. They were dedicated not just to teaching lessons in reading, history, and math, but to helping develop the whole person to become a good citizen.

Along with academics and physical education, our school also taught lessons in discipline and behavior, lessons that I remember very well. I remember at lunchtime, as we opened up our bento boxes filled with cold fish and rice, our teacher would talk to us about current events or give us lessons on morality and how to live a good life.

The lessons were similar to the Christian Ten Commandments: do not steal, do not lie, respect your parents, and things like that. Our parents trusted the teachers completely, and they never questioned their methods.

Another difference between schools in the U.S. and schools in Japan was that Japanese schools did not hire people to take out the trash, sweep the floors, or clean the bathrooms. The students were responsible for those things, starting in kindergarten.

At the end of the day, when each student had finished cleaning up, we would line up and wait for the teacher to inspect our work. If the teacher wasn't happy with the job, all the boys would have to stand up and form one long line facing the teacher. The boy at the front of the line would go down the line, slapping each of the other boys, until he reached the end, then he would take his place at the end of the line. Then the child who had been second in line would do the same thing, and this process would be repeated until each child had gone down the line and everyone had been slapped equally.

I was always glad that this group punishment was only applied to the boys, but this type of public humiliation ensured that we all did our jobs with the utmost care, with perfection. The only job I did not care for was cleaning the bathrooms. I really didn't mind any of the rest. I enjoyed a nice clean school, so I was glad to do my part to make it that way.

At home, however, my siblings and I didn't do any household duties because our family had two housekeepers who lived with us. One was responsible for most of the housework, while the other did all the cooking. Every Japanese family that was middle class or above had domestic workers at that time. It was considered part of your duty to help provide jobs for those who needed work. It was also a sign of a respectable family.

My siblings and I spent much of our time at home studying at our desks. At night, I put my navy pleated skirts under the mattress to keep them pressed, and in the morning, we put on our ties and combed our short-cut hair exactly the same way. When it was time to go to school, we all walked together—not just my brothers and sister and me, but the whole neighborhood. An older student would be designated the leader, we all met at a specific spot on a street corner, and we walked the 30 minutes to and from school together every day.

Our parents did not have to worry about taking us, we were all one big group, and we took care of each other, like one big family.

JAPAN

Part II

WHEN I WAS GROWING up, my parents really dictated how much free time my brothers and sisters and I had. Even during the summers, we still had homework due at school, dance lessons, swim lessons, calligraphy lessons, and daily physical education on the sports field. When our work was finally over for the day, and we were able to play, my mother set a timer, and we walked outside into our garden. We knew our time was limited, that soon the timer would go off and mother and father would call us back in, but for those precious minutes, we were unsupervised and truly free.

I cherished every moment of it. Being outdoors was so wonderful to me. The sandbox, pull up bars, and swing that my parents had put in our garden became like a playground for the whole neighborhood. Friends from school would sometimes come and play games with us, but I didn't need a lot of girlfriends because I could entertain myself so easily. I could climb to the very top of the giant Banyan trees, higher than all the others.

Sometimes on the weekends, once our lessons were completed, my parents would let us wander the countryside just outside of town. I loved to catch butterflies with my little net, or cross the hills and walk down to the beach, or play in my grandfather's huge estate, which was always so much fun. There was a large manmade lake with gazebos around it, and several creeks where I could catch tadpoles and minnows, or maybe even find a few snails.

That is hard to imagine now, a girl of 8 or 9, playing in open fields or walking over a mile by herself to the beach, but that was the kind of world we lived in. We felt very safe. There was very little crime, and children were taught how to be responsible for themselves. But this was before the war. Everything we knew would change very soon.

The Shock of War

The Japanese school calendar is a little bit different than in the U.S., and because Taiwan was under Japanese rule and we attended a Japanese school, we followed their calendar. Instead of two terms beginning in the fall with a long break over the summer, their school year is made up of three terms. The first term begins in April and runs through July. Summer break comes next and lasts from late July until the end of August. Then the second term runs from September through December. They end the year with a final term from January through March, and then students are immediately promoted to the next grade, which begins in April.

There was such an emphasis on physical education in the Japanese culture, not just at school, but also in family life. Every morning before the start of class, all of the students had to gather in the sports field to hear the principal make the day's announcements. After that, one of the teachers would stand up on a big platform and guide us through an hour of morning exercises. This was all before we even began our classwork. Then, over summer vacations, every morning the neighbors would gather in the street, and one person would lead the entire neighborhood through a daily exercise routine. Everyone was welcome to join, children and adults of all ages.

That is why, when we were all called to the sports field in the middle of the day in December of 1941, I thought we were going to do some special group exercise or training class. When the principal announced that we were at war with the United States, I could not have been more shocked. War? Why were we at war? I thought the war was on the other side of the world.

I was not too worried, though. I had seen the Japanese soldiers in parades, walking around Keelung, and at my grandfather's estate. The Japanese army was using the estate for some kind of special defense purpose, so I knew they were strong, they were disciplined, they were healthy, and they would win.

The war was all over the newspapers. I remember reading that the Japanese Air Force destroyed American Navy ships on the Hawaiian Islands, and then quickly took over the American occupied islands in the Pacific Ocean, including the Philippines. This all just confirmed my faith in the Japanese forces.

Every day at lunch, our teacher would sit with us and discuss what was happening in the war. My calligraphy was perfect, just like the printed form, so I became the designated class reporter. I was only 9 or 10 years old, getting ready to enter the third grade, but I got up early every single morning and caught up on the war news of the day. Then, before class started, I pushed a chair up close to the blackboard, stood on top of the chair, and wrote from my notes the details of what I had read. I chose the stories that I thought were most important, such as how many bombs the Japanese army had dropped, how many U.S. airplanes had been destroyed, things that showed how strong the Japanese forces were and how well they were doing in the war. Our newspapers didn't say too much about how many Japanese planes had been shot down, or anything negative like that, so it was pretty easy for me to choose the right headlines.

While we ate, the teacher went through each thing that I had written. As we talked, she passed around a little bowl for us to put discarded rice husks and leftover food into, ever the resourceful Japanese citizen, collecting feed for her chickens. She also often used this time as an opportunity to knock the Chinese for fighting alongside the Americans and the Soviets in the war.

Even though I never felt like she personally discriminated against me, I could never forget my grandparents' Chinese portraits hanging on the wall in our home. I could never forget that I was really Chinese. It really bothered me a lot, but I never said a word. I just swallowed it. I didn't even tell my mother.

The Japanese forces may have made significant strides early on, taking over island after island in the Pacific Ocean, but as the war progressed, things started to turn. The U.S. forces became more invasive and kept getting closer and closer to Taiwan. We began to have air raid practice at school and in the neighborhood where we lived, so the people would know what to do in case of an attack. During the drills, when we heard the loud, rapid air raid siren blast, we had to run home as quickly as possible and get into our homemade shelters.

The northern city of Keelung, where we lived, was the first city in Taiwan to be bombed. I was sitting in class the first time we heard the sound we had all been practicing for. We had all experienced the air raid drills, but hearing the blast during an actual attack was terrifying. As the loud noise rang out, the streets quickly filled with people running in all different directions. So many of my classmates were crying, as even the youngest school children were trying to make their own way to a shelter. It was so chaotic, with people and children running everywhere, and so loud with crying, sirens, and bombs.

As the air raids became more frequent, we learned how to identify American planes in the sky. When we saw a B29 bomber coming, or we heard the very distinct short loud warning signal, we had to run home and get in the shelter.

The Japanese government had ordered everyone in the cities to build air-raid shelters inside their homes, and if the raids happened at night, we were instructed to cover all of the windows with black cloth, so the enemy could not see the residential areas from the air. We did not have any idea how to really protect ourselves from the bombings, so our shelter was pretty simple. My father made it out of a big log and some type of black tarp, which was the only thing we had that was large enough to cover all of us. My parents put it right in the middle of our house, so when we heard the sirens, all we had to do was get underneath the tarp. This was pretty effective at protecting us from falling debris, but the U.S. planes were dropping incendiary bombs, which were designed to cause fire. Japanese houses are made mostly of wood, so they burned very easily. Our makeshift shelters were not enough protection.

So, then we built a shelter outside the house, in the garden, and built it into the ground. And at some point, the school built a couple of very large air-raid shelters in the mountains behind the building. Since shelters only had one way in and one way out, my biggest fear was that the bombs would cause enough falling debris that it would cover the entrance, we would not be able to get out, and that I would be buried alive.

The government also ordered the citizens to dig water storage retainers into the ground to help put the fires out. At first, my family dug ours in the floor inside the house. Then the government said everyone must dig a reservoir in front of their house, so anyone could have access to it, and all the women (because they were typically home during the day) practiced drills of getting water from the retainer and using it to put out a fire. We were told that the only way to stop the fires from spreading is if we all worked together, no one concerned with only their house, but everyone pitching in to help everyone else.

But the water reservoirs caused some unexpected problems. Accumulated water, it turns out, is a breeding ground for mosquitoes, and soon malaria and Dengue fever began to spread throughout the city. Everyone started using mosquito nets at night while they were sleeping, and we were told to look for mosquitoes with dots on their wings because they were the ones that carried the malaria virus. Whether this was true or not made little difference because all of our efforts had only a limited effect.

So many people died from diseases, not just mosquito-borne illnesses, but also smallpox, typhoid, cholera, and tuberculosis. We were constantly getting new vaccines, but they just could not keep up with the spread of disease. I ended up contracting Dengue fever. This virus infection is sometimes called the 21-day fever because the symptoms usually last for about three weeks, but it is often fatal. Many people in my town had already died from it.

Being cut off from China and much of the rest of the world, medicine, like everything else, was in short supply. My father's third oldest brother,丁瑞魚, was a doctor, though, and he was able to get the quinine pills I so desperately needed for my treatment. Even though I was very sick with temperatures as high as 104 and I hardly left my bed for several weeks, thanks to the medicine, I eventually recovered. I was one of the very lucky ones.

When I returned to school, I picked up my job as the class reporter again. By this point, though, it was becoming increasingly difficult to find anything positive in the headlines to write on the board. The U.S. planes were taking off from Chinese air bases, which gave them a big advantage in the region, and they began taking back more and more of the Pacific Islands, which had been taken by the Japanese forces early in the war. The bombings on Taiwan were happening even more frequently, and things were getting very scary very fast.

Early in 1943, when I was in the fifth grade, I read one morning that the U.S. Air Force was planning to drop a different kind of bomb, one that could completely destroy whole factories and important buildings. They had been dropping leaflets in cities warning the citizens of the coming destruction and advising them to move away from large cities, out to the villages and countryside, in advance of a large-scale attack. I could not believe what I was reading! Why would our enemy warn us? Why would they be so kind? That sort of thoughtfulness would never have entered the minds of the Japanese Imperial Armed Forces. It was my first experience with that kind of mentality and my first idea of what the American people were like.

Choosing to heed the warning, and knowing that our large brick home would likely be a target, our family decided to move to my father's hometown of Lukang, in the central part of Taiwan. My father had to stay behind in Keelung, with all the other men, as part of the self-defense team. So, my mother packed all of our things, and all five of us small children, and got on a train bound for Lukang.

Everything was so chaotic and scary. We were part of a mad rush to get out of the city, and everyone was fighting for space. People were climbing all over the train cars, trying to climb in through the windows, and I was so frightened that I would get shoved around and lost in the crowds. But I didn't, and we made it.

Escaping to Lukang

Before it was all over, we would end up spending two years in Lukang. I really got to know a lot about my father's ancestral home during that time.

Lukang was pretty much the same as it had been when my father grew up there. It was a small, isolated village with very few schools. I enrolled in the small all-Japanese grade school; there were only eight students in the class! There was no middle school in Lukang, though, so my older brother had to ride a train to a school in a nearby city.

The schools weren't the only thing that was different about Lukang; the people there still followed traditions that were considered outdated in more modern cities. Some older women had bound feet, and people still chewed betel nuts, which are seeds from a type of palm tree. You could easily pick out someone who chewed the highly addictive seeds; they stain your teeth a telltale deep red or purple.

Most houses in Lukang didn't have things like running water or indoor plumbing. My mother, siblings, and I moved into a two-bedroom house just outside the village on some farmland that belonged to one of my uncles. Considered a vacation property, the house was small but nice. We all squeezed into the two tiny bedrooms to sleep, and there was a maintenance man who lived on the other side. We got our water from the common well, and we all used the common toilet, which was nearby. We used a bucket in our room as a toilet during the night.

At that time, we didn't understand that having the public toilet so near the public drinking water was bad. I had constant diarrhea. There were other practices that we did not realize were bad at the time, too, such as the farmers using human waste as fertilizer to grow their food. But nobody really worried about that. The thing we were all afraid of was tuberculosis. We did not have any medicine for it back in those days, and it killed many people. I remember the marriage matchmakers would not make a match for anyone with a known family member who had "the lung disease." That is how scared of it everyone was.

People didn't know as much about diseases back then. I remember one lady who lived close by used to come over to borrow our pots and pans or different cooking utensils, things I am sure she could not afford or did not have room for in her own house. She had black marks all over her body and her face always looked swollen. Later, we learned that the woman died from leprosy. We were told that leprosy is not easily passed from one person to another, so the chances of us getting it from sharing cookware were very small. But we worried about it for many years and watched our bodies for symptoms of the terrible disease. Thankfully, none of us ever showed any.

Even though our family lived in the small vacation house, the rest of my father's family all lived in the same large complex that his ancestors had built years before. The entire complex was built in a circular pattern around a large well in the center, a common area where everyone could wash clothes and wash dishes, a shared outhouse, and a semi-outdoor bathtub. Then, in the common prayer area facing the square in the center of the complex, there was a Buddhist shrine where the family members could pray and dedicate food as an offering. On the wall, there were photos of my ancestors.

All of the male heirs lived in the complex with their respective families, each one having only one or two small bedrooms for their whole family. Including my father's three older brothers, one of their male cousins, and the widows of some of the deceased male heirs, there must have been at least 30 people living in the family complex. I have no idea how they all lived in such small spaces, 9 feet by 9 feet bedrooms no bigger than the size of a bed, with only a curtain for separation. One family had six children and only two bedrooms! But they figured it out somehow. They must have sat around The Square, the common areas in the center, to have conversations, and went to their rooms only to eat and sleep.

Everyone spoke Taiwanese, of course. I'm not sure how I conversed with anyone there; I suppose it was all that language I had absorbed from listening to my mother talking to my grandmother and aunts. I had learned just enough to get by. I understood their questions and just shook my head or used hand gestures to respond. Even though we could not communicate very easily, the Lukang family was very happy to have us there. Because of the distance between the two places, Keelung and Lukang, we had not seen that part of our family much and this was our chance to get to know each other.

In Asian culture, children do not address elderly people directly anyway. I would never have walked straight up to one of my elders and called them by their name. In fact, we always talk about our older relatives by how we are connected to them. Even in the way we address people, we honor their place in the family. For example, I remember calling one of my relatives Eighteenth Aunt. That is the name I used when I spoke of her. I hardly spoke to her because she did not speak Japanese, but whenever I saw her, I gave her a familiar smile.

The War Comes to Lukang

Even though we were out of the city, we were not completely away from the war—and the fears that came with it. We still saw airplanes fly over, and we still had air raids. My uncle built shelters for us in the ground outside our little house. He built them by shoveling a whole lot of dirt on top and then building a little house-shaped structure on top of that, so it was kind of like double protection. There was still only one way in and one way out, though, and I never quite got over my fear of being buried alive.

The American forces began targeting supply chains and firing at the trains that ran through Lukang in an attempt to stop the possible transport of war materials. During this time, there were a lot of air raid sirens. I vividly remember a particular day when the air raid sirens sounded while we were in the school. The very first thing I did was try to find my younger sister who was in the second grade. When I finally found her, she was just standing there crying. I grabbed her by the hand, and we ran home as fast as we could, with my sister crying the entire time. As we ran, the planes flew so close to the ground I thought I could reach up and touch them. The sound of the machine gun was enormous and horrific.

I will never forget how afraid I was. I was certain that I would be killed. Later that day, we found out that the man who lived across the street from us had been shot in the shoulder riding on the very same commuter train that my brother took to and from school every day. My mother was so nervous that my brother had been hurt and waited all day for him to come home! Thankfully, he had not been on the train that was shot, but my mother never got over the fear. From that day on, she'd watch for his train to come home every afternoon.

We also struggled with food shortages in Lukang. There was never enough food to go around, and the longer the war went on, the worse things got. My father was still back in Keelung, and he only came for the occasional visit. We didn't have a lot of cash, so my mother began exchanging pieces of our clothes for food. There was a lady who picked oysters and sold them on the street, and my mother traded with her. She also traded with fishermen, but with the constant air raids and machine guns, fishing was very restricted. When we were able to do so, our whole family would all go down to the beach and scrounge around to see what we could bring home. The caretaker of the grounds, the man who lived on the other side of our house, planted a vegetable garden for us, so we always had that, if nothing else.

We did what we could to make our food last longer and to make do with what we had. We didn't have refrigeration, so we pickled a lot of our food. We'd made a porridge out of our rice and ate it with a little bit of pickled fish or pickled vegetables and soy sauce. I remember waking up in the mornings with puffy eyes and swollen hands and feet. Now I know it was all those salty, pickled foods. It was a really bad diet, but it was all we had at the time, and it kept us alive.

Surviving the War

Sometime in 1945, our beautiful house in Keelung was directly hit with a bomb and completely destroyed. My father was still in the city, but thankfully not at our house. He said nothing was left but a hole in the ground. My grandfather's estate had been being used as a headquarters for the Japanese Army, and somehow it had survived the attacks mostly untouched. But our house was gone, and I never saw it again.

Later that year, we learned that the United States had dropped a bomb on Hiroshima, a very large city in Japan, and that one bomb wiped out the whole city. We later found out it was an atomic bomb, but at the time I could not imagine such a thing. The force of that bomb must have been incredible, something we had never seen before. But Japan did not surrender. A few days later, the U.S. leveled another entire city, Nagasaki, with another atomic bomb. The whole city, completely gone, just like my house. Even still, it took another five days for Emperor Hirohito to surrender.

For Japanese people, the surrender was very shameful. Our soldiers felt that they had disgraced their families and their country by losing the war. For many of them in higher ranks, it also meant that they would be assassinated or forced to commit suicide to save their family's honor.

Military-style training begins in grade school, with the public slapping and shaming for not doing your job perfectly. For Japanese soldiers, surrender was not an option, and they were expected to fight to the death. That is the reason so many U.S. prisoners starved to death in Japanese war camps. The Japanese soldiers never expected to take prisoners; it was a complete shock to them when the American soldiers allowed themselves to be taken alive. They barely had enough food for their own military; they certainly didn't have enough to feed all of these extra prisoners of war.

When the war was finally over, Taiwan was given back to China as part of the peace treaty. Japanese occupation was all I had ever known.

All of a sudden, we were Chinese again.

My father was happy. He was cheering the end of the occupation, and the end of the discrimination we had endured as ethnically Chinese Taiwanese citizens. But my mother was so sad. She had so successfully adapted to the Japanese culture, and done such a thorough job of instilling it in her children, that for her it was a big loss.

When the Chinese government came back in and took control, they seized quite a lot of property, including the Yen family estate. Today, the gold mine is a museum and there is a single brick made of pure gold locked inside a glass case at the entrance. One of my Yen cousins is currently in charge of maintaining the remaining portion of the Yen estate. He even uses the fresh mine water to raise sturgeon to sell to restaurants.

This left us in a strange predicament after the war was over: Our house in Keelung had been destroyed, and we had nowhere to live and nothing to return to in Keelung. But my father had a plan. He had gotten a job as the head of the state department on trade, and he moved our family to the capital city of Taipei.

I've often wondered what would have happened to us if we had somehow lost my father during the war. I suppose we would have managed, but my life would have turned out very differently. I'm really not sure how any of us survived. We went through so many things, bombings, machine guns, dysentery, Dengue fever, rampant disease, and hunger. I guess I'm just a survivor.

Many years later, long after I had moved away from Taiwan, my father's ancestral home in Lukang also became a museum. The Ting family complex was designated as the Provincial Heritage Home of Ting Imperial Scholar after my great grandfather, and it is open to the public. I took my children and my grandchildren there when they were little. I showed them their unique heritage and showed them how our family made it through the war.

Chen Dai's 陈埭 *Ting Ancestral Shrine was announced by the State Council as the National Important Culture Preservation Unit on May 25, 2006. The stone tablet was set up by Fujian Provencial Government in June 2006.*

Announcement by the Fujian Provencial Government on the Ting Ancestral Shrine as the Cultural Relics Protection Unit in June 1983.

Visit with the grandkids to the Ting Ancestral Shrine in the city of Jingjiang in the Fujian Province.

The names of Ting's 14 Imperial Scholars listed in the Ting Ancestral Shrine. My great grandfather was the last Imperial Scholar on the list.

Visiting the Ting Ancestral Tomb in the city of Jingjiang with the grandchildren.

Ting Ancestral Tombs in Jingjiang.

Altar of Lukang Ting Ancestral Residence. A travel guide site explains: "The Dings arrived from Fujian in the 1820s, and within three generations were established in the upper echelons of Lugang society. The family enjoyed tremendous prestige after 1880, the year in which Ding Shou-quan 丁壽泉 passed the highest level of China's imperial civil-service examination and became a jinshi (進士, "presented scholar"). He went on to become a renowned tutor. A red and gold tablet bearing the two Chinese characters and thus signifying his status is fixed high above the doorway to the central chamber. Inside, the family's ancestral shrine is flanked by photos of Ding scions and their spouses."[1]

---

1   "Ding Mansion," *GuideGecko*, http://www.guidegecko.com/taiwan/monuments-buildings/ding-mansion/p,608185893.

The sign to the entrance of Ting Scholar's Ancient Residence in Lukang, Taiwan.

Joe and I at the Lukang Ting Ancestral Residence with my second cousin who manages the Residence, my granddaughter, and my grandson.

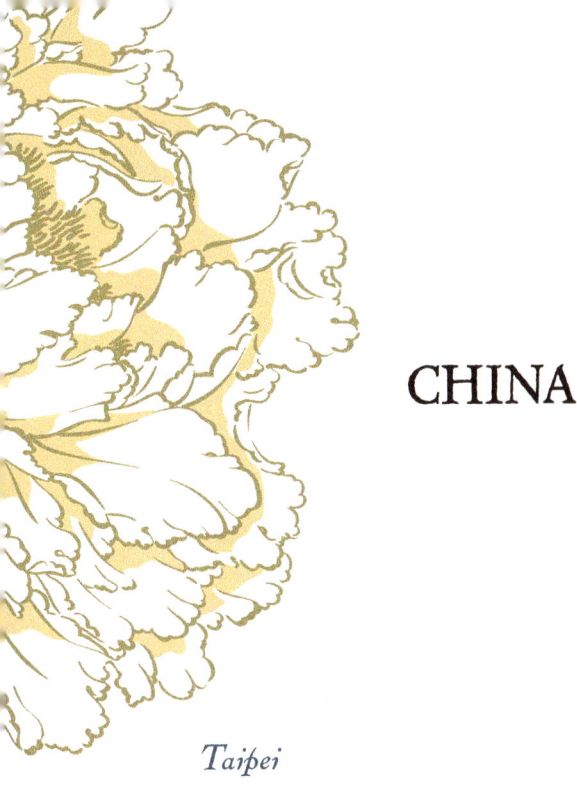

CHINA

Taipei

WHEN OUR FAMILY ARRIVED in the capital city of Taipei in late 1945, everything was in chaos. The newly established Chinese government had ordered the immediate evacuation of all Japanese citizens. All of their public property was seized, their personal property had to be sold, and they were only allowed to take with them what they could carry. Everywhere we went, we saw Japanese people trying to sell as many of their possessions as they could for cash. Everything that they couldn't sell or carry with them—household items, clothing, small furniture—had to be given away, sold, or thrown away.

My father bought several exquisite pieces of Japanese furniture from some of his close friends, although he did not do it out there on the street. He saved them some bit of dignity, I suppose, and made the deal in private. I am certain they appreciated knowing they had sold their precious belongings to a friend, someone who would appreciate them. I am so thankful that he later shipped several of those precious antiques to me. I still have them in my home today.

As the Japanese population hurried to sell their precious possessions and leave the city, Chinese people began arriving in large numbers. In fact, so many people came from China that it created a housing shortage. Even with all the newly vacant homes, there were too many people and not enough places for everyone to live. We managed to find a house in a good location owned by a kind Japanese family getting ready to go back to Japan. It was very chaotic, trying to find a place to live, so in order to secure the house, our whole family moved in with them before they left. The seven members of my family occupied the living room and one small bedroom, while the four members of their family took the rest of the house. We just all squeezed in there together.

But not everyone managed to find a home in Taipei, occupied or not. Many of the Chinese soldiers were simply living on the streets. I remember thinking how different they looked from the Japanese soldiers I was used to, with their impressive uniforms and their disciplined, militaristic demeanors. The Chinese soldiers were wearing shabby uniforms and cloth shoes, and they carried their pots and pans and other belongings on bamboo poles slung over their shoulders.

There were also American soldiers in the city. Some were recently released prisoners of war and some had been sent there to help ensure a peaceful transition of power. I remember seeing them walking around the streets of Taipei, buying all kinds of things from the relocating Japanese families. This was the first time I had ever seen an American. I could not believe how tall they were, and their noses were so pointed! And they were so disrespectful! I saw one solider buy something and just throw his money at the Japanese gentleman who sold it to him.

It was so pathetic to me, watching these highly respected Japanese families reduced to peddling their possessions to rude American GIs as the shabby-looking, homeless Chinese military took charge.

I wondered what kind of world we were going to be living in.

Second Girls' Middle School

Children in Taiwan do not attend schools according to where they live like they do in the U.S. Instead, students take a test and then are assigned

THE ROC

In October of 1945, the Nationalist Party in China, also known as the Kuomintang (KMT), led by the sitting president, Chiang Kai-shek, set up a Republic of China (ROC) government in Taiwan. Many of the Taiwanese people, like my father, thought the Chinese were liberators from the harsh Japanese rule. They had high hopes that control of Taiwan would return to the Taiwanese people. Those hopes were dashed fairly quickly, though, as the ROC immediately sent Kuomintang officials from mainland China to assume all of the highest level government positions in Taiwan.

As the dissatisfaction of the Taiwanese people grew, tensions with the Chinese government officials eventually escalated to a boiling point. A seemingly minor incident on February 28, 1947, triggered an uprising that would last for decades. When KMT officials accused a widow woman of selling contraband cigarettes and then publicly beat her, it sparked local outrage. These protests were violently put down by the KMT, and thousands of civilians were killed. In response to the uprising, the ROC instituted a long period of martial law in Taiwan. Quietly, however, this was also the birth of the Taiwan Independence movement.

Tattered by decades of civil war, ill-equipped to deal with expansion, and susceptible to corruption, the ROC found itself in trouble back in mainland China, as well. The Chinese Communist Party (CCP), led by Mao Zedong, seized this opportunity to capitalize on what they saw as apparent weakness and kicked off the Chinese Communist Revolution.

When the ROC eventually lost the war to the CCP in 1949, Chiang Kai-shek and all of his Nationalist Government officials were forced to flee to Taiwan. Kicked out of China, but still claiming to be head of the Chinese government, the ROC took a stand the only way they knew how, by firmly establishing themselves as the rulers of Taiwan. Taiwan, under control of the ROC, separated itself from Mao Zedong and communist China. So, the union between mainland China and Taiwan never really solidified. In the 1980s, after the death of Chiang Kai-shek, the ROC slowly began to loosen its grip of absolute power on the Taiwanese people. Then, through the continued work of the Taiwan Independence movement, further political and social liberalization eventually led to the first free election of a Taiwanese president in 1996. It was an event 50 years in the making, and I never thought I would see the day.

a school based on their performance. I tested high enough to attend the First Middle School, which was the highest-rated school in Taipei. But with the move from Lukang, my mother wasn't able to submit my forms in time. Instead, I went to the Second Girls' Middle School, the second-highest rated school in Taipei. The teachers there were top-notch. Our school principal even graduated from Yale University!

Attending school in Taipei made one thing very clear to me: Japan was gone from our lives. The Chinese government wanted to show that their education system was superior, so everyone had to learn not only Chinese but also English (which the Chinese considered to be the universal language) and Taiwanese. I was no longer allowed to speak the only language I had known for 13 years, the one I had been forced to read, write, and speak with absolute precision. It was not easy learning all of these new languages at once, and I had to take an extra conversational Taiwanese class for a short time. It was such a strange feeling, being forced to speak a language that I had not been allowed to utter previously. Even now, when I speak or hear a group of people speaking Taiwanese, I have this feeling deep down that we are doing something we shouldn't.

Even my name changed: I no longer went by *Tei Jun Ji*, the Japanese pronunciation of my name. In my new school, I was known as *Ting Chwen Erl*, the Chinese pronunciation.

There are similarities between Chinese and Taiwanese, but the pronunciations are very different, so learning them at the same time had its challenges. In Mandarin, not only do you have to roll your tongue just right, but you have to use the right intonation. For example, the word for the number four is the same word for death, but the intonations are different. Even still, hotels there do not have a 4th floor, similar to the way many hotels here in the U.S. do not have a 13th floor—it's just superstition.

One time, I was going to buy a cotton blouse in the shopping district. The words for cotton and noodle have almost the same pronunciation, which is "mian," but the intonation and written characters are different. So, I was walking around the shopping district asking person after person for a noodle blouse and no one could help me! Finally, someone figured out what I was trying to say, and after laughing a few minutes, helped me find what I was looking for.

To help my parents catch up and adjust to the new languages, they paid to have Chinese tutors come to our home. Although we children were studying Chinese in school, Father requested that all of us join in their tutoring sessions once we had finished our homework. Conversational language in Taiwan began to be a mix of so many languages: Japanese, Taiwanese, and Chinese. I also joined five or six other students for English classes with a group of Benedictine nuns at the University of Taiwan. It was the most intense period of learning in my life!

I quickly acquired a tight-knit group of six girlfriends from school. We all had to take the same courses: history, geology, mathematics, physics, Chinese, English, physical education, and morals. We were all together all the time, and we were all under the same pressures, which I think added to our sense of community.

There were seven of us who went everywhere and did everything together, so we started calling ourselves the Seven Friend Team. We even dressed alike: Students at Second Girls' Middle School all wore the same uniform, but my friends and I also had the same shoes. I always wore a straw hat to protect my face and head from the sun, so my friends started wearing straw hats too.

All of the members of the Seven Friend Team rode the bus to and from school together. For me, riding the bus wasn't necessary. Our house was within walking distance to the school. But I wanted to spend more time with my friends, so I asked my mother to buy a monthly bus ticket for me. It was kind of an expensive request, but my mother understood that I wanted to be with my friends, so she let me do it. Instead of walking one direction to get to school, I walked the other direction to the bus stop. I got on first, and as we rode along, we picked up each of my girlfriends.

Getting on the bus first carried a lot of responsibility. There were so many Chinese coming from the mainland, and the schools were overcrowded. Sometimes there would be 50 or 60 students in a class

I am sitting in the middle of my middle school classmates, all of us in the girl scout uniform and with the same hair length, which were part of the school rules.

with one teacher. The buses were also overcrowded. Since I got on the bus first, it was my job to save seats for all of my friends. By the time we got to school, there would be people hanging off the doors and windows. There were no regulations. If you could get on the bus, even if you were just holding on to the side, you could ride. If you couldn't, you had to catch the next one.

About six months after the war ended, something incredible happened in the Ting family. My third uncle, my father's third older brother, was a doctor, and had lived in Singapore for many years. He enlisted in the Japanese Army when the war broke out and had been "Missing In Action" for a long time. We thought he must have been killed since the war was over and we still had not heard from him. Then one day, he suddenly walked into my father's office in Taipei, and the story he told was unbelievable. In fighting for the Japanese on one of the South Pacific Islands, he had been captured

Testing Boundaries

The language wasn't the only thing that was different about attending a Chinese-style school. There were a lot of differences between Chinese and Japanese culture, too. For example, the principal of our school was a woman, and the vice principal was a man. It would have been unthinkable in Japan to have a woman in a higher position than a man, and there were no female Japanese executives. Women mostly stayed and worked at home. This was really eye-opening for me. I was living in a different world. There were a few more freedoms, and things were a little more relaxed. I didn't feel as much stress.

I even started to rebel a little bit.

First, I asked my mother to make my skirts longer than the standard length. When no one said anything about that, I asked her to make them gathered rather than pleated. When no one said anything about that, some of my friends started to wear their skirts the same way I did. Then, over the summer, I let my hair grow longer and did not cut it back to the required short bob before school started. That's when the dean of the school finally said something.

Actually, that's when she *did* something. On the very first day of class after the summer break, the dean walked straight over to me with a pair of scissors and cut my hair off, right there in the middle of class. I didn't say a word. I just smiled. It didn't bother me. But she was very upset and sternly told me that during the school term I must keep my

---

by the U.S. Army and taken prisoner. But instead of going to a prison camp, he ended up working for the U.S. Army as an English translator, since he spoke both English and Japanese. After the war was over, he was released with all of the other prisoners of war and sent back to Taiwan. With a little help from the arrival harbor, he was able to find where my father worked, make his way to Taipei, and find his office. My uncle was very lucky, and the entire Ting family was both shocked and elated by his return.

hair no longer than the regulation 1-inch below the earlobe. She also mentioned the length of our skirts and made us all change them back. Then, she had a long talk with me and my group of girlfriends about hanging out with each other too often and gave us a lecture on the benefits of mingling with other people.

Again, we just smiled. We knew they were serious about the rules, and had severe punishments including expulsion for committing three 3rd degree infractions. But after the Japanese occupation and the war, after everything we had all been through, we could handle this.

The Seven Friend Team started testing our boundaries in other areas, too, and finding more and more opportunities for freedom. We started taking trips together, and it felt like freedom to us. The family of one of the team had a summer cabin, so we would go there and sometimes we would even stay overnight! My parents were somewhat strict, and they did not always let me go, but sometimes they said yes, if they knew we were going to be someplace safe.

Thinking back now, my parents must have been so happy that I had such close friends. They did so much to help foster our relationships. They would often have food delivered to us, while we were off on some outing. Once in a while, my father would even come to the school and just watch us through the glass windows, while our classes were in session. At the time, I thought it was a little unusual. After becoming a parent myself, I think I understand that he just wanted to see me interacting in the world, to know that I was okay. And I was okay. My friends and I were bound together in such a way that we rarely fought. When one or two of us had a disagreement with another, the rest of the group rallied together to help find a resolution and make peace. Even now, all these years later, although I've lived out of the country for most of my life, and three of us have passed away, the remaining four see each other as often as we can and are still deeply connected.

One member of our team had an uncle who owned a movie theatre. On Saturday afternoons, once we got out of school (we had a half-day of school on Saturday during the school year), she would take us all

Taiwan middle school classmates—six of the Seven Friend Team, after one passed away.

to see a movie for free. We went every Saturday and we saw all the newest releases. That is when we started getting our first real glimpse of life in the West. I especially loved the movies with tap-dancers like *Singin' in the Rain* with Donald O'Conner, Gene Kelly, and Debbie Reynolds. I knew all the well-known movie stars' names by heart, especially other tap-dancers like Leslie Caron, Fred Astaire, Ginger Rogers, and Cyd Charisse.

Around the same time, an American library opened up near our neighborhood, and that is when I really became familiar with politicians and movie stars of all kinds. My father would stop by there on his way home from work and pick up a copy of *The New York Times*, *Life Magazine*, or *Time* magazine. I don't think he read very much of them, but I did. I ran to him as soon as he walked through the door, before he could even take his shoes off, and grabbed the magazines from under his arm. I read about the war from an American perspective, which was so different from what I had read and reported on in grade school.

I also read the wedding announcements in the New York Times, so big and so fancy, and nothing like what I saw in the Chinese newspapers. I read everything I could get my hands on, from cover to cover. It was simple enough language that I could understand it, and it really helped me practice my English.

The more I was exposed to American culture, the more I noticed that American things seemed to be very enjoyable, and thought I might like to go there sometime.

One day, in 1949, something fascinating happened. An actual senator from the United States of America came to our school and spoke to the students. Senator William Knowland was a strong supporter of the Nationalist Government in China and our principal invited him to visit our school. Even though we were all taking English courses, we were not fluent in the language, but our principal translated his speech for us.

I could not believe it. An American senator came all the way to Taiwan. That really made an impression on me.

LEE

My first younger brother Lee was a really smart kid. He is about two years younger than me, but only one year behind me in school because he took a test and was able to skip the sixth grade, and from fifth grade went directly to junior high school. He was always really small for his age, but once he skipped a grade he was even smaller than the other kids in his class, and he started getting picked on once we moved to Taipei. There was no anti-bullying campaign back then, and the kids picked on him pretty hard. In retaliation to all the bullying, he started hanging around on the streets and getting into fights. One time, he beat up an elderly person pretty badly, and my mother was really upset about it. I'm not sure I had ever seen her that upset about anything before. When he got home, she made him bow down and pray for forgiveness in front of the altar for my ancestors.

Walking the Middle Road

Even though I only had six years of Chinese education, I have the fondest memories of that time. We had the very best teachers from China and my favorite courses were the Chinese language courses. I always loved languages—Japanese, English, Taiwanese—but I loved Chinese the best. Our language coursework involved translating the classic Chinese philosophical theories and proverbs, which were written in the classic writings by philosophers like Confucius (551-479 BC), Laozi (sixth – fifth century BCE), Mengzi (372-289 BCE), and others from the fourth through the sixth centuries. We did the translation, and our teachers explained their doctrines. To this day, some of those doctrines are still guideposts in my daily life.

In fact, one of the concepts I learned in middle school that I still try to live my life by comes from the Confucius doctrine known as the *Mean*. *The Mean or the Golden Mean* is written formally with four

---

I was a pretty typical older sister, so every time he and I got into an argument after that, I would taunt him about it: Remember when Mom embarrassed you and made you bow down in front of the altar? One time my mother heard me doing it and she gave me a spanking so bad, I never did that again. I was in high school, but she still spanked me for it. Since she had been such a highly respected teacher, it was extremely disturbing for her to hear me bring that incident up again and again.

Today Lee, once a tough street kid, is a retired Boeing aeronautical engineer. He has many health issues: chronic pain, mobility problems that require him to walk with a walker and drive a car with extra features for handicapped people, but he is taking care of his daily life all by himself. His voice is still strong, and he is always cheerful, just like when he was young. When I listen to him talk, I can tell that, in spite of everything he must go through on a daily basis, he still has a positive attitude about life. He inspires me so much.

Chinese characters 中庸之道, and is pronounced *Zong Yong Zhi Dao*. In English, zong yong is "the mean" and zhi dao is "of the road." The term speaks of a general middle of the road policy, the middle course, a happy medium. It advocates impartiality, reconciliation, and compromise.

One explanation from *China Knowledge* is:

> The concept of 'the mean' is a core idea of Confucianism. It says that in all activities and thoughts one had to adhere to moderation. This would result in harmony in action, and eventually in a harmonious society. Pure harmony without wandering from the central tone (an image from the field of music), and standing in the center without leaning towards one side would keep all social positions stable. A man in a high position must not be arrogant, otherwise the people would rebel. Simple-minded persons in high position must not think of their own profit, otherwise the social structures would be disrupted.[2]

That is just one of the many explanations for and interpretations of this doctrine. When I sat in class, listening to the teacher's lectures, I interpreted it very simply to myself as, "If you walk in the middle of the road, your life will be peaceful."

I believe that to this day. Take the concept of money, for example. You don't have to spend your life making lots and lots of money, but you don't want to be poor, either. The key is to walk in the middle road. You may find that you can make a lot of money going one direction, but that direction will require sacrifices to be made in other areas. For example, my father made a lot of money working for Mr. Wang's plastics company, but he sacrificed his happiness to do it.

You have to decide whether or not it will be worth it. If you do nothing and find yourself in poverty, you've gone too far in the other

---

[2] "Zhongyong 中庸," *China Knowledge*, http://chinaknowledge.de/Literature/Classics/zhongyong.html.

direction. But if you stay in the middle road, not swinging too far to the right or to the left, life is calm. It is amazing that a 2,500-year-old proverb is still so applicable today, but this thought has really been with me and helped me through my life. Maybe this idea of the "middle" is how I ended up choosing a college.

All the schools in Taiwan were overcrowded, but the universities were particularly crowded. The best-rated nationally-funded schools were the hardest to get into, of course, and since I knew that a college education was the key to my financial future, I started looking at my options. I had heard that some of the Catholic nuns who taught my private English courses would help students apply to schools in the U.S., so in 1952, just before I was about to graduate, I asked my parents if they would let me study abroad.

At that time in Asia, most parents were not really concerned with making sure their daughters received higher education. Sons' education was the first priority. Not only was I asking to go to college, but I was also asking them to spend a lot of money to send me to college out of the country, so I was making a big request. But my mother was an accomplished educator herself, and she worked with my father to make the decision. To my great surprise, my parents, who often would not let me stay overnight at a friend's house, actually said yes. I was ecstatic. I could not believe it. So, I went to Sister Ronayne, the Benedictine nun, and told her that I wanted to apply to go to school in America.

"Where in America would you like to go?" asked Sister Ronayne. She might as well have asked me where on the moon I would have liked to go!

I thought to myself for a minute and said, "Well, I think I'd like to go to the middle of the U.S."

I looked at a map of the U.S., put my finger down right in the middle, and landed on Kansas. I had never heard of Kansas before, but the state had a nice rectangular shape, which I liked, so I said, "Sister Ronayne, help me find a school in Kansas."

That is how I ended up applying to Mt. Scholastica College in Atchison, Kansas. Sister Ronayne helped me get the entrance permit and a scholarship from the school, but that was just the beginning.

The Taiwan Ministry of Education also required a Chinese Constitution Exam, and a high school transcript; the U.S. consulate required a security deposit of $2,000, and the trip fare was around $800 USD. That was a huge sum of money at the time.

My parents never said *"I love you"* when I was growing up. In our culture, people did not express their emotions verbally that way. In fact, it was seen as kind of childish. But I never doubted my parents' love. They made it clear over and over again, in every little thing they did for us, every little sacrifice. This time was no exception. In order to come up with all the money we needed to send me to America, my father sold a large piece of farmland that had been part of my mother's dowry, and that supplied all the necessary funds. I may have been only 19 years old, but I was about to have a very big experience.

It was all very stressful—the details of the application process, everything needed by the different governmental agencies, and coming up with the money. I really did learn a lot about taking care of myself through this process, but the tremendous pressure was starting to get to me.

Before I left for college, I decided to take one last English course over the summer. My course was taught by an American woman, the wife of an engineering company representative living in Taipei. The U.S. Government had sent a bunch of technical people over to aid in the developing the Taiwanese economy, and they had built a large complex where all of the company employees lived.

It was the first time I had seen western architecture, and the first time I saw a western toilet. When I walked into the washroom, I had never used anything other than a squat latrine, but I saw this big white seat sitting there. I looked at it closely, wondering why someone would want to sit on the same seat where other people had sat. Deciding that was unsanitary, I climbed up on top, carefully positioned my feet on either side of the seat, and squatted down over it. My feet kept slipping, and I was so unsteady I almost fell off. I wondered how many other things were going to be so different for me once I arrived in the U.S.

My departure to the U.S. Front row: My parents and me. Back row, left to right: my first younger brother, Lee; my younger sister, Eileen; and my second younger brother, Elon.

Leaving Home

The day I left for the U.S., my father took me to the airport in Taipei. After we got my ticket and walked over to where my plane would be taking off, I realized that I would be flying on a large DC-6 piston-powered plane. I was so nervous, and I started to feel a little sick to my stomach. It was the first time I had ever left my parents. I looked at my father, with concern in my eyes. My father was so stoic, and he just walked me to the boarding line.

I got on the plane, and sat down by the window, feeling the most alone I had ever been in my life. When I looked out onto the runway, I saw my father standing there, with his hand in the air. I don't know how he got there, I know he wasn't supposed to be there, but there he was waving at me.

I don't know if he could see me or not, but I waved back, and I didn't stop waving until the plane was so far away I could no longer see him.

I wondered how my parents could let me go. They had always been the most strict of all of my friends' parents. They asked 20 questions just if I wanted to stay the night with a friend. But they didn't ask if those Catholic nuns knew what they were talking about. They didn't know anyone in Kansas. They did it because they loved me, and they knew this was the best choice for my education.

The DC-6 did nothing for my tummy troubles. Within just a few minutes, I was really sick and had to lay down. I was also homesick. I saw some Asian guys on the plane, and they reminded me of my brothers, so I talked to them for a while. The plane landed first in the Philippines, then Guam Island, and then on Wake Island. We stopped for a meal at an American military R & R site. Then we went to Honolulu and San Francisco, and finally landed in Kansas City.

The whole trip had taken a day and a half, but it wasn't over yet. I still had to ride a bus the 40 miles from Kansas City to Atchison. I have no idea how I managed to communicate with the ticket agent, buy a bus ticket, and get on the right bus, but I did.

It was August. It was so hot on the bus, the food was all so new to me, and I was really homesick. I was physically and emotionally breaking down. When I looked out the front window of the bus, all I could see was a long, straight, flat road. There was nothing to the right, nothing to the left, and nothing but road straight ahead.

Well, this is the middle of America, I thought to myself.

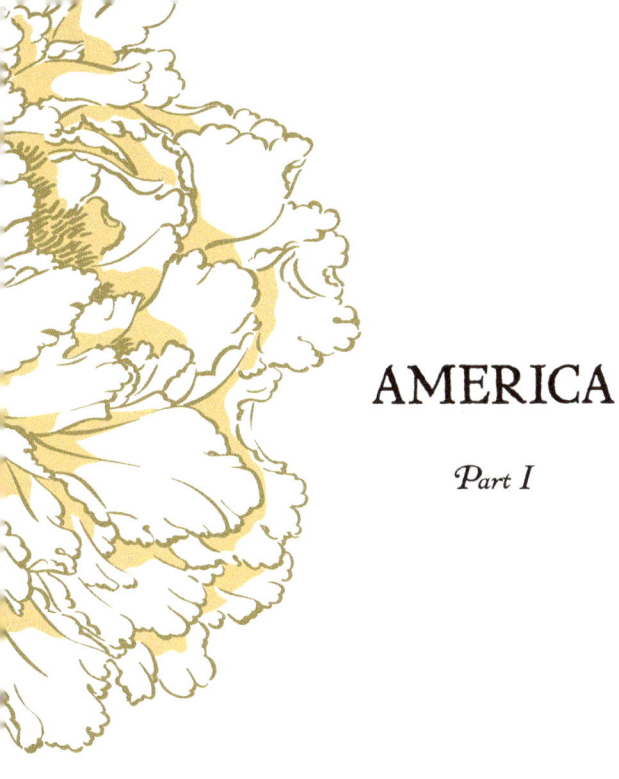

AMERICA

Part I

I SPENT MY FIRST FEW days in America in the school infirmary. The trip had been a long exhausting one and Atchison, Kansas, was so different from any place I had ever been. It was sparse, not like the cities where I had grown up, the food was completely different, and I was having a hard time adjusting.

It didn't help that I arrived at The Benedictine Sisters of Mount St. Scholastica College two weeks before the semester started, which meant that most of the other students were still home, enjoying summer break with their families. I spent my time reading, walking around, and trying to get more familiar with the place. I eventually met a few other students – mostly from Hawaii or parts of Asia – whose families lived too far away for them to go home over the summer. Many of them had found part-time jobs working in the kitchen.

I'd visit with my new Asian friends in the kitchen during the day. In the evenings, I'd return to the big, empty dormitory, which was one big room with about 45 unoccupied beds. The beds were separated by privacy curtains that formed little "rooms." In addition to a bed, each room had a small dresser with a mirror and a chair. There were also lockers in the hallway; one for each girl.

Of course, there weren't any other girls – not yet. I missed my home. I missed my six girlfriends; missed being part of the Seven Friend Team. My older brother was in Seattle attending the University of Washington there, but that was so far away, he might as well have still been in Taiwan. I was so homesick and lonely that I went to the bathroom and cried for hours. I received letters from my parents, but I was so sad I could not even read them. I just stacked them in a box unopened.

Mount Scholastica was run by the Benedictine Order and I found myself visiting the nuns on campus whenever I felt especially sad. They were such dedicated teachers, and always tried to encourage me and give me advice; they reassured me that it takes time to adjust. The nuns were a source of comfort to me and I learned so much from them. It was during these visits that the idea for my new American name began to take shape.

My Chinese name, *Chewn Erl*, is really hard to pronounce in English, and I kept having to correct the nuns. Eventually, a nun called Sister Marie suggested that I choose an American-sounding name, one that would help me fit in a little better with my classmates.

I liked that idea: a new name that fit this new place, this new phase of my life. I had a Japanese name and a Chinese name, so having an American name made perfect sense to me. All I had to do was choose a name I liked.

But what would I choose?

I went back to my empty dorm and thought about the names of the American movie stars I had read about – but I quickly decided that I didn't want to pick a name I had seen a lot in magazines. I finally decided on Joyce. I remembered reading that name on a list that Sister Ronayne had given us back in Taiwan, and I thought it was pretty; I liked it even more after I found out that it means "happy." I wasn't feeling happy just yet, but maybe the feelings would come with my new American name.

As it turned out, I did start feeling happier. At night, my Asian friends in the kitchen would sometimes cook Asian dishes and invite me to join them. That helped a lot. Before I knew it, two weeks had

Freshman classmates of Mt. Scholastica College, Atchison, Kansas in 1952. I am in the very right of the second row from the front.

I hosted a Mt. Scholastica College reunion in Seattle in 2009.

passed, and the rest of the students finally returned to school. I looked around this new place and saw so many people, so many possibilities to make new friends.

I still missed my home and my family, and I missed being a part of the Seven Friend Team – but it was a start.

Dorm Life

It was hard to feel truly alone once the semester started. The huge dormitory – the one that had felt so empty when I arrived at Mount Scholastica – was suddenly filled with students, American girls. It was the perfect opportunity for me to really see what American culture was like.

The first thing I noticed is how loud the American girls talked! They were so animated, and opinionated, and talked with each other even late into the night. And they smoked! Outside of bar workers, I had never before seen a woman smoke, so that was very different.

The American girls also loved music. Many of them had personal radios and played music in the evenings while we were studying. This was when I was introduced to 1940s and 1950s American music. I loved it! Of course, all of the noise, chatter, and music in the dormitory made it difficult to study and get enough sleep – and sleep was important, because no matter how late we had stayed up the night before, we still had to get up and go to Mass every single morning.

I tried my hardest to sleep in. I was not Catholic, and I did not want to go to Mass! But the supervising nun would come into our room and wiggle our toes until we got up. I tried so hard to ignore them, but there was no way. Catholic or not, we all had to go.

Of course, early morning Mass wasn't the only unfamiliar custom I had to adjust to. I'll never forget how shocked I was when I started eating in the cafeteria. There was so much food! It seemed like we had mashed potatoes every single day, a big mound of them covered in gravy right in the middle of the plate. It was so heavy compared to what I was used to. Such big portions and so much starch. On Fridays, they served fish. I remember when I first heard about this, I was excited.

I was used to eating fish every day, and I missed it. But when Friday rolled around, they put this big hunk of thickly breaded something on my plate. I wondered where the fish was. I guessed it must be river fish or lake fish—it was certainly not from the sea. I didn't know why they put so much flour on it. You couldn't even taste the fish!

What shocked me the most, though, was that they served dessert after every meal. I could not believe that. In Taiwan, dessert is only occasionally served as a very light snack in the middle of the afternoon with tea, not immediately after a huge meal. I thought, *who can enjoy this when you are already full?* At first, I gave my portion to someone else. Before I knew it, though, mashed potatoes with gravy became my favorite food, and I ate dessert at every meal, just like everyone else. It did not take me long to catch up!

So many things were different in Kansas. I missed the ocean so much: the smell of it, the breeze from it, swimming in it. One time, it rained really hard and I saw what I thought was a river off in the distance. I ran toward it as fast as I could, but when I got there I saw that it was just a puddle, just an illusion. That winter, I saw snow for the first time in my life. It was so beautiful to look at, almost like white sand that stuck together, but when I went outside to roll around in it, I could not believe how cold it was. I decided to build a snowman because that's what everyone said you were supposed to do. A man from the local newspaper showed up and started taking pictures of me.

Maybe the people in Kansas found me just as unusual as I found them.

Religion

Even though some things got easier during my time at Mount Scholastica, I never felt completely at home there. I was not doing very well in my classes. My English still was not very good, and even though I studied a lot, I was struggling to keep up in almost every course. Except for my dance class, for which I had earned an A, I was getting Cs and Ds in all of my other classes. Even though my teacher advised me against taking another language class when I was not fully mastering

English, I really wanted to take Spanish, and signed up for it the second semester. I ended up doing better in that class than any of the others.

The thing that I struggled with the most, though, was religion.

I had gotten used to going to Mass every day, but as the year went on the school's emphasis on Catholicism had become a cause for concern. It started with my friend Martha. Martha was my one good friend at Mount Scholastica. She was really nice, and she talked a lot. It was easy for me to be around her, so we started eating our meals together and hanging out all the time – until suddenly, one day, Martha was just gone. She was not in the cafeteria. She was not in class. I could not find her anywhere. And then, I found her: It was a Sunday, during high Mass. I walked into the church and she was sitting up front with the nuns, which meant that she had become a novice, or a nun in training. I had no idea Martha was even considering that!

I was sad to have lost my friend, but I was also starting to worry. What if they forced me to become a nun, too?

Then, in the middle of the academic year, it was announced that the entire student body had to go off campus for some kind of religious retreat. They took all of us to a Catholic encampment and for four days we did nothing but go to Mass and attend special lectures. Instead of regular schoolwork, we were supposed to read our bibles during our downtime. I went to Mass and did the bible reading, but I assumed the lectures were optional, and since I wasn't Catholic I didn't go. I just went back to the room. That next week, when we all got back to school, I was called to the nuns' office and officially reprimanded for skipping the lectures. I did not realize that attendance was required. They had been taking names at the door and I was counted as absent, just as if I had skipped class.

I was at Mount Scholastica on a scholarship, so the reprimand worried me: Would I lose my scholarship for not attending the lectures? But it also worried me that the lectures were mandatory in the first place. Were they going to force me to become Catholic? What if they tried to force all of us to become nuns, like my friend, Martha?

I have to get out of here! I thought to myself.

I am so glad that I was not raised with any particular religion. I had a lot of discipline at home and at school, but religion was something different, and I feel it is not something that can be forced upon someone else.

Back to the Sea

Since Robert (Ting Yih-Min) 丁逸民 had already paved the way in Seattle, when I asked my parents if I could visit there, it was not a very difficult decision for them to make. They would at least have two of their children in the same place for a little while.

When summer finally rolled around, I was so excited to go to Seattle and spend some time with Robert. I took a long train ride through Nebraska, Wyoming, and Montana. I really got to see a lot of the middle of the U.S.! My brother was still a student, and had arranged a place for me to stay when I got there, but I quickly realized that I needed to find a summer job. I thought that if I could find work as a babysitter for an American family, maybe I could get room and board rolled into the pay, so that's what I did.

I found a job as a live-in babysitter for a family in Seattle and all that summer I took care of their children. Sometimes in the evening or on weekends, I would hang out with my brother and his friends. There were so many Asian people in Seattle, and Robert had a big group of Asian friends. We all spoke the same language, and ate the same kinds of food, and I especially loved being near the ocean again. This place felt more like home.

My scholarship was already in place for the second year in Kansas, but I decided to write to my parents anyway. I told them that I thought they were going to try to force me to become a nun at Mount Scholastica, and I asked them if I could transfer to Seattle University, where my older brother Robert was, before that happened. To my great surprise, they approved, and I was so happy. The transfer process takes a little while, so I knew I would have to wait one more year before moving, but at least I had something to look forward to.

I saved as much money as I could that summer. I did not want to live in a dorm anymore once I transferred to Seattle, so I knew I would need extra money for room and board. And when I returned to Kansas in the fall, I immediately began filling out and processing the transfer request. As a foreign student, especially one who was on a scholarship, there was a lot of red tape, but I was committed to the process. The good news was that since Seattle University is also a Catholic school, all of my religious courses transferred, and I did not lose any credits. But Seattle University is a Jesuit school, and much more open than Mount Scholastica. There were more freedoms for the students, and I did not think they would try to convert me into a nun.

I did a little better in my classes the second year, but still only managed to get Cs and a few Bs. My heart just was not in it. My heart was already in Seattle.

Seattle

When I got to Seattle, I immediately found another job working as a housekeeper and babysitter, which was perfect for a student. I eventually took a better paying job with the Seattle Library.

Two years later, I graduated from Seattle University with a degree in home economics. Cooking and taking care of a household had always appealed to me. We didn't get to do much of that growing up, since we always had housekeepers, and I enjoyed all of it very much. I considered going on to study Spanish at the University of Washington, but I was already 24 years old, both of my younger siblings were studying in the U.S. by that time, and my brother was still working on his PhD. That meant my parents had four children in college in the United States. I felt like I needed to stop taking money from my parents, who were still paying for my tuition, and become completely independent.

My job at the library didn't pay much, but it was enough that I could get by. So, I set my budget and made a life for myself.

It was around this time that I received my first marriage proposal, which came as a shock. I hung out with a big group of friends, but I

Graduation from Seattle University in 1956.

didn't really date much. So, I was surprised when one of my brother's friends, a Taiwanese student who was part of our group, asked me to marry him! We had never even been on a date by ourselves! So, I said no. I did not really know him very well, and besides, I did not want to marry an old-fashioned Taiwanese guy and live that kind of traditional life. I wanted something different.

My parents and I disagreed on this point, and they tried their best to introduce me to someone, a young man somewhere in the U.S., I don't even remember where, whose parents were still back in Taiwan. He was very popular among the young Taiwanese women; all the parents wanted their daughters to marry him. I wrote to him a couple of times, just to show my parents that I tried, and through our letters I found out that he was a Ph.D. scholar. No wonder my parents liked him. We exchanged a few letters, and in them he told me about himself. Mostly he just studied and went to school, but he also told me that he liked to take a nap every day around 1 or 2 o'clock in the afternoon. That's when I stopped writing to him. I did not want to be with someone who wanted to take a nap every day. How boring! I never even asked how much money he made. It did not matter to me.

I found out later that he was devastated by my rebuff, since he was thought so highly of in my parents' social circles. Everyone else seemed to think he was a great catch, but I wanted something else. I wanted to do something fun with my life.

One of my favorite ways to have fun in Seattle was to go to Chinatown. At that time in Seattle, in the 1950s, all sales of meat and liquor shut down at 6 p.m. I'm not sure if it was part of the blue laws, or if it was a union thing, but they even put paper over the meat and liquor sections in the grocery stores, so you couldn't see the products. But in Chinatown, you could buy anything 24 hours a day.

I started going to Chinatown with one of my coworkers from the accounting firm. Her boyfriend was a performer at a club in Chinatown, and since everything else shut down at 6 PM, she invited me to go to this club with her one Saturday night. She was older than I was, probably in her 40s, and she took care of me, kind of like a chaperone. Everything was so wild down there, people were drinking and smoking, but I loved watching people dance. I still remembered the dance class that I took at Mount Scholastica, the one class I had gotten an A, and how much fun it was.

But my friend warned me not to dance with anyone.

"Just tell them no," she said, so I just sat and watched the others.

Then one Saturday night, after I had gone with my older friend a number of times, I decided I could go down to Chinatown without a chaperone. I knew which busses to take, and I knew how to take care of myself. So, I asked another friend of mine, a girl about my age, and she agreed. I put on my best dress, a white one with a large tiger on the front, and my friend and I went together.

After we got there, I started feeling a little nervous. Everything seemed even more wild and out of control without my chaperone. So, we were just sitting there, watching people, when a young man came over and asked me to dance. I remembered the advice of my friend, *just tell them no*, but this guy looked nice, and besides, I really wanted to dance. So, I said, "Yes!"

He said his name was Joe, and after we had been dancing for a few minutes, he asked for my number. I told him, right in the middle of our dance, and he didn't even bother to write it down. I asked him if he wanted a piece of paper, but he said, "Don't worry, I'll remember it!"

I thought I would surely never hear from him again.

After Joe and I danced, my friend and I got out of there. We hadn't even been at the club an hour, but that was enough. I wanted adventure, but I wasn't ready for that much adventure.

The next morning was Sunday, and I was doing my ironing for the week when the phone rang. To my great surprise, it was Joe! He had actually remembered my number after all. We talked for a few minutes, and then he invited me to go with him to the zoo that afternoon, since it was one of the few things open on Sunday. I did not have any plans, so I accepted, not really sure what to expect. Joe picked me up right on time, and we talked so much, even on the first date. Joe was so easy to be around, and I enjoyed his company very much.

I learned that Joe worked second shift at Boeing, which meant he worked from 3 p.m. to midnight, during the hours that I was off. In fact, the only reason he was even in Chinatown the evening we met is because the only bars open when he got off work were in Chinatown. Despite the differences in our schedules, though, Joe called me every day after our zoo date. He took his "lunch" break at 7:00, and he called me every night at 7 o'clock on the dot.

Joe was extremely punctual and that made an impression on me.

In our conversations, I learned that Joe had been born in St. Paul, Minnesota, but had moved to Grand Forks, North Dakota, when he was 5. His father was a mechanic and, after his parents' divorce, Joe had mostly taken care of his two younger sisters. After graduating from high school, Joe had joined the Navy just as the U.S. was entering the Korean War. During the war, Joe spent two years in Trinidad, but he also spent a little time in California during training. He liked California so much that he had planned to move there after getting out of the Navy, but instead had chosen to follow a friend to the Pacific Northwest. After getting a good job at Boeing, and seeing how beautiful Seattle is in the spring, Joe just decided to stay.

When I first met Joyce, it was love at first sight. I will never forget the image of her standing there in her tiger dress. She was so beautiful. I had never been out in Chinatown before, but my friend talked me into going that night, and as soon as I saw her I was so glad that I did.

I nervously walked over to her and asked her to dance, and to my great surprise she said yes. To my even greater surprise, she was a really good dancer. I got up enough nerve to ask for her number, and when she told it to me I memorized it immediately. There was no need to write it down, I knew I would never forget it.

When I went back to ask her for a second dance, she and her friend were nowhere to be found. I was so disappointed they had left, but at least I had gotten her number while I still had the chance.

I could not wait until the next morning to give her a call, so bright and early Sunday morning, I dialed her number. Lucky for me, she was already up doing her ironing for the week. There were not many things to do in Seattle on Sundays, but I knew the zoo was open, so I asked Joyce if she would like to go to the zoo, and she said yes. That was our first date, but it was the first of many.

~ Joe Marleau

"Do You Intend to Marry Me Or Not?"

Joe did not even have a college degree. He was far from the scholar my parents would have chosen for me, but we had so much in common. You really get to know a person when you talk to them on the phone every day, and every time we opened our mouths, we found ourselves saying the same thing. We liked going to the same places, we liked doing the same things. He was also honest and kind. I was only 24 years old, and did not have a lot of experience dating, but I had never met anyone like that before.

Joe was a gentle person, but dating him felt intense. We talked every day, and he had this little black Chevy, and we went to all kinds of places together. After about a month, I introduced him to my brother Robert and my younger sister, Eileen (Ting Ling-Erl丁玲兒), who was attending the University of Washington studying mathematics by then. When they both seemed to like him, I knew this was the guy I wanted to marry.

The only problem was, I wasn't sure if Joe wanted to marry me. He had never said anything about it. And if Joe had no intention of marriage, then I didn't want to keep going out with him. I didn't see any point in wasting time if he didn't want the same things out of the relationship that I did. I wanted to either get married or end things completely.

So, one night, I just asked him, "Joe, do you intend to marry me or not?"

The look on his face was pure shock. I don't think he ever expected me to be so bold, and as I think back now it really was an over-the-top question. But my boldness helped him to open up and admit to me that a coworker of his had warned him that I might only be dating him for a green card.

Now, it was my turn to be shocked. "I don't need you for a green card," I said. "I have been in this country for five years, and I have a college degree and a good job. I am eligible for citizenship all on my own!"

"Well, in that case, then, yes I want to marry you very much," Joe said.

So, on October 4, 1957, only six weeks after we met, Joe and I

Our wedding on October 4, 1957.

got married. It was a simple ceremony at the Justice of the Peace, with my sister as my bridesmaid and a friend of Joe's from work as his best man. We had a small party afterward, with just a few friends and family, and Mrs. Smith, the lady who owned the boardinghouse where I lived.

I had only told my parents a few days earlier. I knew they would be upset when they found out, and I wanted to limit their suffering as much possible. I came from a family of scholars and they wanted something very different for me than an American with only a high school education. But I knew marrying Joe was right. I knew we could have a good life together.

We didn't have enough money for a honeymoon, so we just went down the street to the first motel we came to on Aurora Avenue. Later that night, we were listening to the radio, and we heard all of this commotion going on. The people on the news were going crazy over the first Soviet satellite, Sputnik, being launched into space. Joe said that was our fireworks.

When we were first married, I probably had more money than Joe did, but I was living in a boardinghouse, and Joe was renting a room from a family. So, we moved into Joe's little room until we could find a place of our own. When Joe came to help me move all of my things out of the boardinghouse, I looked at the little black car we'd spent so much time in. Suddenly, it seemed so small!

"Do you have room for all of my noodles?" I asked.

"Your noodles? What on earth are you talking about?" he said.

"When I was in college in Atchison, Kansas, my father was worried that I would not have enough food to eat, so he sent me cans of noodles," I said. "Lots of them. They are in my closet."

I took him up to my room, opened up the closet door and showed him stacks and stacks of canned noodles and tea, up to the ceiling. I don't think Joe was expecting that! But somehow we made it all fit in the car.

Even without the stacks of noodles, Joe's little room was too small for two people. I started looking for a house to rent. I thought I would feel more comfortable renting from an Asian person. This wasn't easy to find. Even though there were a lot of property owners in Seattle who were Japanese, they did not advertise their ethnicity. It was too soon after the war, and Japanese people were still looked at as enemies by many American people. But I saw this one place, and for some reason I could tell that it was owned by Asian people, something about it told me, possibly my sixth sense. So, Joe and I went by to take a look at it, and when we knocked, a Japanese-looking woman opened the door. When she saw the two of us standing there, an American man and an Asian girl, she just slammed the door in our face. I am guessing she thought I was a war bride—a prostitute who had married an American GI during the war.

That was the first time we felt the real sting of discrimination. Mixed-race couples are a lot more common now, but back then, Joe and I were pioneers.

I have been thinking often about how marrying Joyce affected me greatly. When Joyce became so involved in writing about her life, it made me reflect on my own life.

I come from a broken family, as my parents were always fighting. Finally, when I was 17 years old, they divorced. The judge advised that I was to collect the support money each month from my father because it would give me the opportunity to see him once in a while. That was very stressful, as he always said terrible things about my mother. I was also taking care of my two young sisters. My father was never close to me—just doing all the fun stuff with his friends. After graduating from high school I joined the Navy, and after being discharged, I moved to Seattle and continued drinking and misbehaving, maybe because I felt so unloved.

When we were married, Joyce didn't know too much about this and just was being herself, taking care of the two children and me. After the children left I began to realize that I had improved mentally and physically and through to this day. I am so thankful for the love and care she has given me. I treasured Joyce's parents as I was accepted as their family member.

Just recently I told her that if it wasn't for her love, I wouldn't be here.

~ Joe

AMERICA

Part II

WE WERE STILL LIVING in our little rented house in 1958, a year after we got married, when our first daughter was born. We named her Karen. I had seen the name in a baby book and thought it was pretty. Joe chose her middle name, Denise, after a woman he had worked with some years earlier. We did not ask my father for his suggestion, as Chinese tradition would have required. I suppose we had already made the decision to raise our children like Americans.

We still only had one car, so every morning I got up and got myself and the baby ready for the day. I carried Karen and all of her stuff over to the babysitter's house, which was about a 10-minute walk from our house, then I came back home, got my stuff, and caught the bus to work. When I got off in the afternoon, Joe picked me up in the car, and we drove together to pick up Karen. Once home, Joe watched Karen while I made dinner and cleaned the kitchen. During the night, I got up with her every time she cried, I nursed her, I changed her diaper, and got up the next morning and did it all over again.

It was not very long before I was completely exhausted. In Asia, women do all of the housework and they take care of the children and they never complain, but I was also working 40 hours a week on top of everything else. I didn't know to ask Joe for help, so I just kept going, doing everything. Eventually my body broke down. I had a terrible headache and an extremely high fever. I could barely move. Joe took me to see a doctor and they told me that I had encephalitis and needed to be in the hospital. I think Joe was afraid I was not going to live. Maybe I was afraid of that too. I was in the hospital for weeks, but I did finally recover, and when I came home, I confessed to Joe that I needed some help, and he was there for me. We started working different shifts, so that one of us would be home with Karen while the other one was at work. Joe also started doing more around the house like cleaning and doing laundry.

He had done all of that for his younger sisters after his parents got divorced, so he already knew how and was always willing to pitch in. I had just never asked him, since I didn't have that kind of example growing up.

We decided it was time to move out of the rented house and buy a home of our own. We had been saving as much as we could and found a great little two-bedroom house with a big back yard on Beacon Hill, which was a nice area. It seemed perfect for us at that time, but in just a few years we were already looking for something else. In 1961, our second daughter, Linda Mei, was born and the room our growing girls were sharing was getting too small for them. The yard, on the other hand, was too big: We were spending all of our time off trying to maintain the lawn. We had paid $10,000 for the house, but we were able to get $15,000 when we sold it. That was a really good profit – a 50 percent return – in just a few short years, and that gave us the money we needed to get into something a little bigger.

I looked at a lot of houses. I don't really like moving, and I wanted this house to be the one we stayed in for a long time. And even though I had started a better paying job at the Boeing Company, we wanted to be smart with our money, not strap ourselves into too high of a mortgage, so our budget was fairly low.

Joe and I went to see this one two-story house on a beautiful tree-lined street called Lake Park Drive South. It was in the Mount Baker

District, a really good area, and it looked nice on the outside. Even though it was $21,000, which was a little outside of our price range, Joe talked me into looking at it anyway. Once we got inside, we could see that the owners had not done anything to it in years, and it needed some work. It had a partially finished attic with two small bedrooms on the second floor, and two larger bedrooms on the first floor. The owner's husband was bedridden in the largest one. He was so sick he couldn't even get up for the agent to show us the house. The house also had a basement, which was good, but it was so full of oil heating and cooling units and ductwork that you could hardly move around. When we came back upstairs, and started walking around the property, I noticed with interest that the small yard hardly had any grass; it was mostly rockery. I liked that.

Then Joe pointed out something that I had not even noticed before. "You know where we are, don't you, Joyce? We are right across the street from that park where you like to take the girls all the time."

I had no idea. I had looked at so many houses, I had lost track. I was only thinking about the price, how we could afford the monthly payments, and how far it was from the girls' school. I didn't even realize where we were, but as soon as he said that, in spite of the price and the work it needed, I knew I wanted that house. In fact, I got so excited that I started jumping up and down!

They say that in real estate transactions you aren't supposed to get emotional about a property, but I didn't know that yet. I was so emotional that day, thinking about all the ways this house was perfect for our family. Even though $21,000 was a little bit out of our price range, we had been saving money and I knew that we could make it work. We made them a good offer that day and they accepted it.

As soon as we moved in we started making improvement plans. The house had one story with two bedrooms, an attic with two small improvised sleeping rooms, and a basement which contained the heating system. The first thing on the list was remodeling the basement. I remembered a story about a supervisor I once had at work. She had been forced to retire early because of health problems. After she retired, she had to sell the house she had lived in for years and move to a small town where the houses were less expensive, because she could no longer afford the rising property taxes on her retirement income. She was devastated.

Seeing this sad example taught me a valuable lesson, one that I did not forget. And after living in our house for 10 years and the girls moved out, we were eventually able to save enough money to remodel the basement and turn it into a leasable apartment. During the basement construction, a worker found a partially torn permit on the wall granted from the Seattle Department of Streets and Sewer and he gave it to me. It had the date of 1924 on the permit. That is how I found out when our house was constructed.

After that, we made the attic into a standard second story by lifting the ceiling to add height and extending the wall toward the front of the house to enlarge it. Instead of crowding the space by making two bedrooms, I just made one large master bedroom and turned the rest of the space into a spacious living area with a sofa and chairs. In 2005, I hired an interior designer and told them my idea to remodel the upstairs bathroom to be similar to a Japanese style bathroom with a deep bathtub and a shower without enclosure.

Since the house did not have enough storage, I also wanted to build large drawers big enough to store things like a Costco package of toilet paper. I decided to utilize the space under the sides of the slanted roof to make two levels of 2-foot wide and 2-foot deep pull-out drawers. This was the greatest idea and it solved my storage problem. I was so elated when I found out that a large Costco toilet paper package fit exactly inside one of those 2-foot drawers!

We were so happy with the entire upstairs remodel, and the space fit our needs and personality so well. It ended up being such a unique design that the designer submitted the work to the National Residential Interior Design competition and won first runner-up in the bathroom category. The photos appeared in the September/October 2005 issue of *Southern Accents* magazine. The design also appeared in *The Art of Luxury Living, Designer Baths by Professional Designers, Fourth Annual Edition.*

Seattle house in Mt. Baker district, across from the park. The house was built in 1924, and we bought it in 1966.

The view of Mt. Rainier from Lake Washington near the house.

The tram that was built in the backyard of Seattle house to lead to the garage.

The tram track leading to the garage.

More recently, we replaced all the glass windows and frames with updated technology and material. Then, a few years ago, since we planned to live in this house for the rest of our lives, we installed a tram to go from the house up the hill to the garage around back, an elevation climb equal to the three stories. The tram has been extremely helpful through the years for both gardeners and workers, carrying tools and materials up and down that steep hill. And now, as we are getting older, we use it to bring bags of groceries down from the car. I don't know of anyone else who has such a short 40-foot tram with a roof at their house, but I'm so glad we did it. Now, we don't have to worry about how we are going to get up and down the hill, no matter how old we get.

The house looks very different today than it did in 1924 when it was built, and very different from the day we bought it. But the money we make from renting out the basement continues, to this day, to pay the rising real estate taxes. That is the reason we have been able to live in a beautiful, upgraded, conveniently located place for over 50 years.

When we first moved in, before we did the major remodel, we gave the upstairs bedrooms to the girls. That was their space, and I hardly ever went up there. I didn't want to constantly be yelling at them to pick up their room, so I didn't even look at it. I believe that if you live a good example for your children with things like a tidy house and cleanliness, when they become adults, they will have learned from that and do the same. And in the case of my girls, I ended up being right.

Our girls were naturally well-behaved and obedient, and they did not need a lot of discipline. Karen was a very curious child and liked to go fishing with Joe. Linda was quieter. In fact, she did not speak at all until she was over a year old, but they got along so well with each other. I worked a lot, but when I was off we took advantage of all the activities available to us in the city. I enjoyed being their mom so much. Even though I did not often use a lot of affectionate language, Joe and I showed them how much we loved them in every little way we took care of them, just the way my parents did for me.

Joe's surprise catch with our daughters, Karen and Linda.

Karen with catches from a fishing trip.

On the occasions when our girls did need to be disciplined, I was always the one who had to do it. Joe could never bring himself to even tell them no, much less hand out consequences. I always thought he was just too soft, but after spending time with his parents and his sisters, I started to understand why. Joe had told me about the way his parents fought when he was growing up, and about their divorce, but there was no way for me to really understand that kind of family dynamic without seeing it. When they came to stay with us in our house, though, I saw firsthand what that kind of instability and mistrust within a family looked like. One by one, we ended up closing off the relationships with Joe's family members. We felt like we had to in order to establish healthy and safe boundaries for our own family. I wish that there had been another way, but we did not feel like we had any choice at the time.

We raised our girls to know my family, and they spent a lot of time with their aunts and uncles and cousins in Seattle. My sister, Eileen, was a great help to me when Karen and Linda were little, before she moved to California. She was such a good aunt, and the girls loved her so much. When they were old enough, we took them to Taiwan to meet their extended family, and when they got a little bit older, I sent them to Taiwan all by themselves over the summer break. Even though we were all spread out, we still tried to keep the family together throughout all those years.

One thing we didn't do, though, was teach them to speak Japanese. I was still struggling to learn perfect English myself, so we chose to speak only English at home with our family and our daughters never learned any other language. I regret that now, but at that time there was no real fusion of the cultures. Immigrant families, especially Asian ones so close after the war, were just trying to blend with the American culture as best they could. And, I am happy to say that Karen and Linda never felt out of place. There were a lot of Japanese-American families who lived near us, so the girls fit right in with their classmates and other kids in the neighborhood.

Meanwhile - Back in Taiwan

While Joe and I were raising our family in Seattle, my parents were doing very well back in Taiwan. My father was in a unique position as the head of trade, working for the state department. He was one of the few Taiwanese citizens in such a high-level position, and it was seen as an honor in the community. Working directly with the import/export trade also put him in direct contact with a lot of successful businessmen and with very high-ranking government officials, so he had a lot of connections. One of the big commodities exported out of Taiwan at the time was bananas, which spoil quickly. My father had the power to say which shipments were moved the fastest, and the exporters often tried to bribe him to move their cargo to the front of the line, to cut down on their losses to spoilage. Sometimes they brought him gifts, sometimes just asked him for favors, so my father was seen as quite an important man in Taipei.

This is probably why my father was invited to participate in a U.S.-sponsored program aimed at promoting economic growth in Asia. There had been a lot of changes in the region in just a few short years, and much of Asia continued to struggle after the end of the war. The U.S. came up with a development plan that included inviting prominent Asian businessmen to attend lectures at Stanford University. My father was selected to attend. While he was there, not only did he learn a great deal about business, but he also made some key connections. Among them were: an important businessman from Thailand, the chairman of Irving Trust Bank of New York, the CEO of a very large company, and many others.

Not too long after he returned from that trip, my father was approached by a man named Y.C. Wang. Mr. Wang was the founder and chairman of the Formosa Plastics Corporation, one of the largest companies in Taiwan. He offered my father a job working in his plastics company, but my father initially told him, "No. I'm sorry, but I am not a chemist."

"But, I already have all the chemists that I need. What I need now is connections, Mr. Ting, and that's where you come in," Wang replied.

It took a little convincing, but my father finally decided to leave his job at the state department and take a position with Mr. Wang. One of the first things Mr. Wang asked my father to do was go to the chairman of Irving Trust Bank, the one he met at the Stanford lecture series, and secure a business loan for $2 million American dollars, to expand the business. Borrowing money overseas was quite extraordinary at the time, but my father's prior relationship helped him secure the loan. As a result, that plastics company eventually grew into what is now one of the largest plastics manufacturers in the world.

As the company grew, my father continued to be very successful; he was routinely awarded bonuses, stocks, dividends, and his assets just grew larger and larger every year. In spite of the newfound wealth, though, he always seemed sad to me. Money didn't seem to be very important to my father. I think he was embarrassed that his older brothers had sacrificed so much to send him to a top-notch business school, and instead of owning his own business, he ended up working for someone else. Mr. Wang wasn't even well educated and was rumored to have sold rice on the streets when he was 20 years old. Yet, he was more successful than my father, and that really hit my father's pride.

The money didn't seem to change the way my parents lived. My family continued to live a modest Japanese lifestyle. And as more and more businesses started to come into the area where they lived, my father decided to move out of Taipei, and chose a small town in the North called Shin Peitou, located near some hot springs. He bought a piece of land there, a double lot, moved the entire Japanese-style house from Taipei to Shin Peitou, and built a smaller house beside it on the second lot. My father then built a 5-story office complex where the house had been in Taipei and sold the property. It was in a very good area, close to the business district and the government buildings, and in the highest fashion area near department stores and shopping. It was a very highly sought after area, so it was not difficult to find a buyer.

One thing my father did with his prosperity was to share it with his children. He divided his assets between the five of us, including the girls. This was not usually done in Asia, where typically the family inheritance was shared only among the male heirs, but my mother insisted that my sister and I receive a portion equal to my brothers. My father gave each of us our portion of a large sum of stocks and allowed us to do whatever we wanted to do with it. For me it was a ton of money. I decided to transfer the funds to an offshore bank and keep it until I decided what to do. Eventually, though, I grew uncomfortable with that arrangement and began to worry that someday I may get a big penalty for not paying taxes, so I brought the funds back to the U.S., paid the taxes due, and invested in Seattle real estate.

Starting to Invest in Real Estate

When I grew up in Taiwan, neither the government nor private companies paid very much in retirement benefits, so people had to save their own money to take care of themselves during retirement. Even though I had been living in the U.S. for many years by that point, that had never left my mind. And since Joe and I both had salaries on the lower end of average, I started to think about our future and how we would pay for our retirement.

The first thing that came to my mind was buying a piece of rental property, but we could not afford to buy another house, so I decided to buy a piece of land instead. I thought, it doesn't matter where it is, as long as it is not too far from Seattle and the monthly payment is within our budget. So, I found and bought a 5-acre lot of land on Camano Island, just north of Seattle. During that time, you could not borrow money from a bank to buy an investment property, so we had to negotiate a contract with the seller. We paid a fourth of the selling price upfront, then financed the remaining balance with the seller, with agreed-upon terms for payment.

As time went on, we were able to buy an additional 5 acres, and then a 10-acre lot, all on Camano Island. After 10 years, we sold the first 5 acres for twice what we had paid. Those pieces of land, and the money we made, were the starting point for our future real estate ventures. From there, we gradually began acquiring more and more properties.

I started reading the Sunday newspapers every single week, looking at the real estate ads. There were still a lot of inexpensive houses at that time, especially in some areas, and on my way home from work I would drive by and look at different properties that interested me. The first house I bought was a dinky little place for $25,000. I knew that if we put too much money in it, then we would have to raise the rents higher to cover our investment; so, we put just a little bit of money into it, not much, and then we rented it out. The next property I bought was a duplex for $39,000, and I handled it the same way as the dinky little house—find an inexpensive property, put just a little money into it, and keep the rents affordable. I thought that by keeping the rent low, down where people could afford it, they would want to stay for a long time. Joe was still working 2nd shift, so we worked out a plan for signing paperwork. I took all the legal and financial papers to him during his 7 p.m. break and stuck them through the chain-link fence that surrounded Boeing so he could sign.

Both of these investments felt solid, but I realized that if I was going to take this any further, I needed to have a little more knowledge. So, I studied for and took the real estate agent's exam, got my license, and got on with a real estate company whose offices were close to where we lived. I was only interested in an affiliation with them so that I could have access to first-hand listings and open-houses for my own investment purposes. I was not interested in actually selling real estate as a job. I did help two of my friends find and buy a house, but the broker noticed that I was not actively pursuing other customers and became unhappy with me, so I eventually left the company.

Later, I also took the broker's exam class and got my broker's license. Just having that license made me feel more confident about taking bigger risks, though, and I bought a 9-unit apartment complex with some of the money that I inherited from my father. It was an older building, but the units were large, and it was in a great area called Queen Anne, at the very end of a street. It was the most money I had ever spent on a property, $100,000, but I felt that the investment would pay off in the long run. I stuck with my original strategy of keeping rents low, but also added something else I thought would help us keep the property continually leased—I interviewed the tenants and chose people whom I thought would get along well with one another. If people get along, they are more likely to stay, and the longer they stay, the better for us.

Around this time, I also started combing through the Sunday papers in search of property closer to downtown. One of the things I learned in broker's courses was the wisdom known as "location, location, location." Even though I could not afford anything in the heart of downtown, I decided to try and find something on the outskirts. It took a while, but finally, in May of 1980, one particular ad caught my eye for some reason. When I called about it, though, the agent just gave me some excuse about why I couldn't see it and refused to schedule an appointment with me. So, I just forgot about it, and kept looking. Later that year, in about October, I was looking through the newspaper again, and I came across another ad that caught my eye, so I called the agent and found out that it was the same property I had called about in May. It was listed by a different company this time and had a different description, so I had not recognized it. I thought to myself, *There's something interesting about this place. I really have to see this property!* I told the listing agent that I just had to see it. He tried to give me excuses about it being difficult to set up an appointment, but I insisted. Finally, and reluctantly, he agreed to call the business owner and schedule a showing.

I was under the impression that I would be the only potential buyer present on the day of our appointment, but when Joe and I showed up there were several other agents there. With all of us standing around outside the building, the listing agent finally told us all why there had been so much secrecy surrounding this particular property. The building's current tenant was a private, all-male club. They did not want non-club members inside the building, especially women, the agent explained. They were making an exception for me, but only because I had been persistent and because Joe was with me. I now understood why there were so many agents at the door with us that day— it was not an easy building to view

As we toured the building that day, I decided right then and there that I wanted the property. I knew I had 30 days to talk to my lawyer and come to a final decision, but I already felt very strongly that this was a good investment.

I wanted to meet the seller before signing on the dotted line, so I requested that the agent set up a meeting. The agent told me they usually do not want buyers and sellers talking to each other because quite often it derails the negotiation. But again, because of my insistence, he set up the meeting. In talking with the seller, I found out that he had been planning to develop the property, but his wife got sick and now required constant care, so he didn't have time to be a landlord and had decided to sell. He also told me the building was sound, had a good foundation, and I got the impression that he was an honest person. I was so glad I had the chance to talk to the owner because it played a big part in helping me make my decision.

The tenant had been there for years, and probably did not have very many places where they could run that type of business. The property was close to downtown, which meant that it was only going to grow in value. I also had a feeling that since the owner was selling for personal reasons, we could get it at a good price. I offered them a little less than $100,000, less than what they were asking, and they accepted it.

For the first time since getting into real estate, I was told to hire someone else to collect rents and manage the property for me. I may have owned the building, but the tenants still did not want a woman coming into their place of business. With all of my other properties, I managed those things myself, but this property was different. I knew it would be worth it.

Boeing Layoff

Just as I was expanding my real estate business, Boeing lost a big contract. Joe and I both got laid off in 1970. It was the biggest layoff in the history of Boeing. Engineers were being bumped down to engineer's aides, everyone else was being laid off right and left, and people were moving out of Seattle like rats jumping off a ship! We even remember seeing a billboard sign with a picture of a lightbulb that read, "The last person to leave Seattle, please turn out the lights."

We were okay, though. Boeing paid everyone good layoff packages, we had some money saved, we had a tenant in the basement downstairs, and all of our properties were leased out.

Just prior to the layoffs, I had been working as one of only two engineering aides with a particular group of engineers. Two of them were from the U.S., and the rest of them were all from overseas—France, Switzerland, Canada, Germany, Korea, and India. My job was to draw the diagrams' testing instructions for whatever projects engineers were working on. Today all of that would be done on a computer, but back then it had to be written by hand, and it had to be perfect.

Handwriting sample from my time at The Boeing Company.

WHO'S WHO AMONG
STUDENTS IN AMERICAN JUNIOR COLLEGES

This is to certify that

Joyce C. Marleau

has been elected to

WHO'S WHO AMONG STUDENTS
IN AMERICAN JUNIOR COLLEGES

in recognition of outstanding merit and accomplishment as a student at

Seattle Central Community College, 1970-71

Director

Recognition of my outstanding merit and accomplishment as a student.

I drew on my calligraphy skills from all those years before when my mother sat with me and made me practice over and over again. You could not even tell the difference between my handwritten documents at Boeing and a typewritten page. But sitting there bending my head and writing perfectly for a long time was also back-breaking work, and my neck and arms were always sore. But they sent me to take some basic computer programming classes and let me start to write a few programs for the engineers, too. I really enjoyed the Cobol work. I enjoyed it so much, in fact, that I started working extra hours, without pay, late at night so that I could have time on the keypunch machines when no one else was around.

After the big layoffs, I decided to take the opportunity to get an additional degree in computer science. Seattle Central Community College was offering courses that were the closest to what I had been doing while working with the Boeing engineering group, so I enrolled. I really applied myself, and when I graduated, I was elected to "Who's Who Among Students in American Junior Colleges 1970-71" in recognition of outstanding merit and accomplishment as a student.

As soon as Boeing started hiring back, about two years after the layoffs, I went straight to Boeing Computer Services, newly established in 1971 just as I was graduating, and they hired me immediately. I was even hired back under what they considered "continuing service," so my employment history did not start over. For retirement and pay scale purposes, it was as if I had never left.

They assigned me to a very interesting project called the Minute Man Missile, and I was on the team that wrote the maintenance manual. This was an interactive system, so we had to think through human nature, routine, and logic to write the programs, understanding what steps people were likely to take on a computer screen. We thought about what message to display if a user clicked on the wrong thing, and how best to instruct them through the program. This was all brand-new technology, and brand-new processes, so my head was constantly full of logic and reason. I worked late, quite often because I was afraid the information would fall out of my head before I got back to work the next day.

Receiving the Special Achievement Award from the supervisor at Boeing Computer Services.

This was around the time when computer usage really started taking off within companies. The Boeing Company was one of the big customers of Microsoft at that time, so I attended many computer seminars and listened to the lectures of Bill Gates, the principal founder of Microsoft. It was a very interesting time with all of the new technology that was emerging.

Joe, in the meantime, decided to open his own business. He had worked for a long time in the machine shop building the templates that make airplane parts, but a couple of years prior to the layoffs he had gotten a position making model airplanes to fly in the wind tunnels. It was a really good job, and he enjoyed it because it was artistic and interesting. He really put a lot of himself into that project; it was like his baby. Then, one night he went to work and everything was just gone. The whole area had been completely cleaned out without any warning. Joe was deflated. He felt like all the work he had done for the past few years had been for nothing. They kept him on a little while longer, but he was literally sweeping the floors just to have something to do.

That is when Joe started looking for something else he could pour his heart into, something that would give him control over his work product. The first thing he did was talk to a neighbor friend of ours who was in the import/export business. This fellow imported specialty items from Japan, things like bamboo rakes and fishing poles, and sold them to outdoor shops. Then he exported Washington-canned fruit back to Japan in big barrels. He was quite a good businessman, and kept up on all the current trends in small business. He told Joe that the big thing was wine-making supplies, and that there was a store right in our neighborhood. He and Joe went down to look at it, and talked to the owner who said he was looking to open a second store, a franchise. They ended up working out a deal, and that's how Joe got into the wine business.

Joe stayed in business with this partner only for about a year, then went out on his own, establishing Cellar Wine-Making Supplies, a company that sold wine and beer making equipment. During that time in Washington, we were not allowed to sell any alcoholic beverages in the store because only state government-owned stores were allowed to sell alcohol. But people were allowed to make their own beer and wine at home, up to 50 gallons per year for household use only, so Joe's store not only sold the supplies, but he was also very busy giving wine and beer making classes in the store.

Later, when the laws were changed legalizing the public sale of alcoholic beverages, Joe started operating as a wine merchant. He attended many wine tastings at the local wineries, and learned how to taste wines himself. Then, in addition to wine and beer making classes, he started hosting tasting sessions in the store to increase the knowledge of wines for both himself and his customers.

We went to Europe and visited many wineries in France, Italy, and Spain, and we got to see the farmland where they grew the grapes. When we were in Spain, we joined the U.S. wine salesmen's tour and visited the winery of the well-known Spanish Royal family, where they presented us with a performance of the Flamingo dance.

It was just a wonderful time in our lives. I don't even drink! I think Asian people are really sensitive to alcohol, or at least I am, so I never drank the wine, but Joe and I both loved every minute of it. He was so happy to be in business for himself and getting to travel only made it even more interesting and fulfilling for both of us.

Teenagers

Our girls were older by this time, giving us the freedom to travel by ourselves. They were also getting less and less interested in traveling with us, since they had their own friends, activities, and social lives. In fact, by the time Karen was a senior in high school, her social life actually started to become a problem. She had gotten excellent grades during school, all the way up through her junior year, but then something changed. At the time, the system allowed students to use their junior year's credentials for acceptance into college, so many students, once they found out they had been accepted, did not have any motivation to study during their senior year.

Without our permission, she started staying out late with her friends, coming and going whenever she wanted, and pushing her boundaries with our authority. I had a really hard time with this. Even though we raised them very differently than either one of us had been raised, with more freedoms and a more relaxed American lifestyle, this was more than I could take. I stayed up late every night, waiting for her to come home and wondering if she was okay. Then I had to get up at 5:00 the next morning and try to be alert all day at work. When I found out that she was also skipping classes at school, that's when I said enough is enough. It was the hardest thing I have ever done, but I told her that if she was going to keep staying out late and skipping school, then she could move out and live on her own. I could not believe how quickly she packed up and left. Just like that, she was out.

One of her friends came to our house and really had it out with me. He was so upset on Karen's behalf and couldn't believe that I had told her to move out. He didn't understand that this was the hardest thing

I had ever gone through in my life, and her moving out had completely broken my heart. It broke Joe's heart, too, but I didn't know what else to do. She had a job at a restaurant making a little bit of money, and I hoped maybe they would also give her some food, so I thought she could get by.

This was during the time when the government had just started a bussing initiative to help desegregate the school system. Recently, Karen told me that there were a lot of students coming in with serious social and economic challenges, and the quality of education at the time was less than ideal. It was no fault of the teachers. The school was overcrowded and there weren't even enough books for all of the students. She confessed to me that she skipped classes because she felt that attending them was pointless. She never compromised her goal to graduate with honors. She completed the highest math, biology, and chemistry classes that her school had to offer, and did well enough on her college entrance exam (SAT) to graduate with honors.

I did not realize any of this at the time. I was struggling with raising teenage daughters, and did not have good communication with her. I now know how much she accomplished in spite of all the challenges.

She managed to finish her last year of high school while working and living on her own and decided to study Pharmacy in college. But when she started attending the University of Washington, she soon found that it was impossible to take a full course load and work, even part-time, to make ends meet, so she decided to move back home.

Later, she was able to work as a volunteer at the Swedish hospital, and that's where she met another volunteer worker by the name of Michael Coe. They soon became best friends and aspired together to be accepted into the University of Washington's School of Pharmacy, with an internship at the Swedish Hospital. While they worked to accomplish these goals together, best friends eventually became boyfriend and girlfriend. They both received their BS in 1981, followed by their Washington State pharmacy licenses. Then, together, like they had made so many other decisions, they decided to change directions and study dentistry and medicine. They studied together for their dental and medical entrance exams while doing their pharmacy internships and both were accepted! Karen chose Northwestern University in Evanston, a suburb of Chicago, because they offered her a full academic scholarship. Michael chose Chicago Medical School. They both passed the Illinois pharmacy licensing exam, and Karen worked part-time as a pharmacist at Northwestern Hospital to help pay living expenses.

A few months before graduating as a DDS and an MD, Karen and Michael got married in 1985.

Linda, on the other hand, was never any trouble in school. She was always a very independent child, with a lot of her own ideas. When she was in middle school, she had a group of really close friends, and all of them were well-behaved and courteous. Our family always enjoyed it when her friends would come over to visit. Linda was also very artistic. She made quite a few interesting ceramic sculptures, and she was so talented that I still have many of them displayed around the house.

Linda attended the University of Washington for one year before leaving to study art and design at our community college. She was always artistically gifted, so she started to look for a job where she could express her artistic talent and interest. She was so happy when she was able to find her ideal job at the City of Seattle working as an engineering designer. She worked her entire career for the City of Seattle, and she enjoyed it very much. As a design engineer, she provided the engineering designs for the signals, street lights, paving, and roadways. Then she accepted a position performing engineering design tasks for the signal operation department and did an excellent job. For her accomplishments over the years, she received an award and many letters of appreciation and praise from her co-workers and project managers.

Several years ago, Linda took an early retirement and is now enjoying a more leisurely life in her beautiful Seattle home. She is delighted to see the roadway, signal, and lighting projects that she worked on are all still in place. And whenever I am driving, I always look up at the traffic lights, and I think of her.

Ama and Akon

One day when Karen's children were very young, she and her husband were visiting us for a few days. I looked over at Karen sitting on the couch, and I could see she was deep in thought. I wanted so much to ask her what she was thinking, but chose to let her have her privacy. A few weeks later, I received a Mother's Day card from her in the mail. She wrote the most heartfelt message inside.

"I am grateful for the motherly love you give me and my family. We are fortunate to have you in our lives. You are an inspiration in your lust for life."

She wanted me to know how much she appreciated my love and generosity toward her family. Karen has always been a really great mother. She has always been devoted to her children and all of her children excelled because of it.

Karen and Michael have two daughters named Erica and Lauren, and one son named Ryan. The kids call us Ama and Akon, the Chinese names for grandmother and grandfather. Just as soon as they were old enough, Joe and I started taking them on vacation with us. We took them to China, Taiwan, and Europe. I always had to negotiate with my daughter for more time with them, so I started the negotiation asking for three weeks, knowing I would probably end up with two. Eventually, though, she agreed to let us have them for three weeks over the summer, and we always had so much fun with them. It was good for them for so many reasons, but it was good for us, too. They lived in Bend, Oregon, so we didn't get to see them every day, and these trips were our chance to really spend some quality time with them. Ryan, especially, was so attached to his mother that at first he called her every single day. By the end of the three weeks, though, he hardly called at all. He had learned how to be calm and enjoy new experiences. Maybe he was learning something about walking down his own middle road. I like to think that, anyway, to think that some pieces of me, pieces of Taiwan, are being passed down to my children and grandchildren.

On a trip to Italy with the grandkids in Piazza Del Duomo, Florence.

On a trip with our granddaughters, Erica and Lauren, in Amsterdam, in the Netherlands.

Two directions to climb China's Great Wall.

Climbing to the top of the Great Wall China with grandkids Lauren and Ryan.

My granddaughter Erica Coe's wedding in 2016. From left: son-in-law Michael Coe, daughter Karen, Joe, me, Erica and her husband Jesse Hollander, daughter Linda, granddaughter Lauren, and grandson Ryan.

AROUND THE WORLD

Japan

ONE DAY IN THE 1980s, I got a phone call from my cousin in Taiwan whom I had not been in contact with for many years. He said that he had gotten a phone call from a Japanese grade-school classmate of mine, Tohara Shigeko. She had seen my cousin's name in the grade school name book, and thought it might be my brother. She called him trying to get in touch with me, and gave him her name and phone number.

When I heard the name, I had to reach back in my mind, way back over 40 years, to recall any memory of her from my childhood. All the memories of that time gradually surfaced. Miss Tohara had been one of my best friends. She lived next door to my house, and we played together just about every day. Suddenly it occurred to me that I might not be able to speak Japanese as I had when I was young! After the Second World War, I went through the six years of intensive Chinese education, with English also required, so I worried if I would even be able to remember Japanese.

I waited a few days before returning her call. I tried to figure out how I was going to apologize if I was not able to speak proper Japanese. When I finally called her, and heard her voice on the phone, it was such an incredible experience that I started speaking Japanese, although it was a little awkward. Simply hearing her voice triggered my memory, and after a few minutes of conversation, I no longer felt that there was such a big gap of time between us.

As we talked, the language started to come more and more easily. Soon, I was speaking Japanese as perfectly as I had as a child, as if I had never stopped. She told me they had held class reunions for many years, ever since they went back to Japan after the War. She said that I should come too, that they would all really love to see me. I could not believe it! I had not seen any of these people since the War, since before my family moved to Lukang. They had all been sent back to Japan, and I never knew what happened to them.

I immediately started making plans to go to Japan for the next reunion. I couldn't wait to see everyone, and to find out what had become of them, what their lives had been like, but mostly I was excited to see my friend. She and I decided to meet in a town called Atami, near the hotel where she worked.

I got off the train in Atami, at the lower level of a department store, and as I ran through the kimono fabric section, I was suddenly hit with the strong scent of the fabrics. I had to go to the corner, place my head against the wall, and close my eyes to recall what the smell was. More thoughts of when I was in grade school gradually surfaced, and I remembered the smell from the casual kimonos, made with blue dyed fabric, and worn by so many women. That smell was still deep in my memory.

When I went up to the entrance of the station to see my friend for the first time in over 40 years, it was such an emotional meeting, we just held our hands for a while without saying a word. She looked just the way I remembered, except for her gray hair. She had been my closest friend from those early childhood years, the one who played with me in the giant Banyan trees in my parents' front yard. Seeing her again was like coming home.

When she took me to her hotel and entered the tatami living room, she suddenly knelt down on the floor and bowed her head touching the floor without uttering any words. I knew right away why she bowed.

Miss Tohara Shigeko 戶原成子, *my best Japanese childhood friend and grade school classmate. We met for the first time in the 1980s after about 40 years after the Second World War.*

She was apologizing to me. After the War, most of the Japanese people became more worldly and realized how discriminatory and brutal they had been toward other nations, especially to Chinese, and Shigeko san was not an exception.

Without saying a word I just lifted her up and we sat down together and talked about what our lives had been like after the war. We talked about our children, we talked about our husbands and our jobs, and about everything we had each been doing for the past 40 years. We got all caught up. She told me that she worked at a resort in a hot springs area. She told me how much she had loved playing in the park at my grandfather's estate when she was a little girl and how most of the Japanese people who lived in Taiwan during the occupation still felt like Taiwan was their home.

Then, I went to the reunion for the very first time with her. I was so emotional seeing the rest of my classmates after so many years that

I was speechless. The reaction was the same for them. As they always did at the reunions, one by one each person stood up and told everyone what was happening in their lives. I was so overcome with the emotion; I could not get through my whole story. I just covered my teary face and sat down.

We have a class reunion two times a year, in June and October, organized for many years by a classmate, Mr. Kanno Tadashi. Since I first started to join them, in the 1980s, I have not missed a single one. I could never thank Mr. Kanno enough for doing such an excellent job of organizing it for us for so many years. After each one, he made sure to update everyone's information and send it out to all of the class members, attaching all the photos that he had taken. In 2018, we were informed that Mr. Kanno unfortunately had a serious health problem and was no longer able to attend the reunions. So one member decided to make June 2019 the final reunion for the nearly 50-year-old class of Hatachi Kai of Futaba Grade School.

Some members said to me that we can still have an informal get together if I would still be able to come to Japan. Not everyone is still alive, others can no longer attend because of health problems, but I will continue to make it a priority. I do not know for how long I can do it, but I've decided to keep going as long as I can, to meet up with whomever else is still able to get together.

Class reunions are very important in Japan. So many times, before we all got up to leave, we would stand up together and sing our grade school song. I was always so moved by the spirit of togetherness that has remained amongst my classmates. As a rule, the Japanese really stick together. It's that mentality, we are one, that made my friend apologize for what her country had done. It is also the same mentality that made them such a strong enemy, a strong army, strong enough to defeat China and Russia, huge countries compared to them. They stick together for life, and they consider me one of them.

When I look back on my life, although I am genetically Chinese, and have been in the U.S. for nearly 70 years, I feel my soul and spirit are very Japanese. I think the pressure of growing up in the Japanese envi-

Biannual Japanese grade school reunion.

Getting together for the biannual Japanese grade school reunion.

ronment, and of my mother wanting me to become a perfect Japanese student and girl during that period, might be deeply rooted in me as a person. I am very surprised quite often, even now, wherever I go and meet people, even in Taiwan, people think of me as a Japanese.

Taiwan

I remember the first time Joe and I went to Taiwan together in the early 1960s, after we got married. It was after my parents had sold the property in Taipei and moved their house to Shin Beitou, which is a small hot springs town outside of Taipei. We traveled all around Taiwan, seeing this family here and that family member there, introducing everyone to Joe, my husband. My parents were traveling everywhere with us, and my father, as usual, was taking care of all the traveling expenses. One day, we were at the airport, and he was buying tickets to fly from one little town to another. My father told the ticket agent he needed tickets for himself, his two grandchildren, his daughter, and his son-in-law. When the agent said the ticket for the son-in-law would be more expensive than the others, since he was not a family member, my father changed his order.

"I'm sorry. What I meant to say was that I need tickets for myself, my two grandchildren, my daughter, and my son," he said.

That's when we knew that my father had accepted Joe as a son. He also got a better price on the plane ticket!

My parents' house in Shin Beitou was in an area known for its many luxury resorts and natural hot springs. Hot spring baths have a lot of health benefits, which makes them popular vacation spots and tourist destinations. But for the people who made their homes near the springs, there were some definite drawbacks: The Sulphur in the water was bad for the plumbing system in my parents' house and the pipes required regular repairs. When my father got sick—he had colon cancer and then suffered a stroke—my mother was there taking care of him all by herself and the maintenance of the house was too much for her to handle. As soon as my siblings and I found out about the situation, we all got together and made the decision that our parents should go to stay with my younger brother, Elon, in the Philippines. My mother needed help and none of us could go stay in Taiwan with them. Elon had a large house, where they would be comfortable, and a staff of servants to help take care of both of our parents. We all agreed to share the expenses. It made the best sense at the time.

Elon is the only one of us who stayed in Taiwan until he graduated from college. He did eventually come to the U.S. for graduate school at Stanford University. After he graduated, he was living in Portland, Oregon, where he got a job with a paper mill company. The company had a branch office in Manila, Philippines, and eventually Elon was transferred there. A few years later, when the company decided to pull their interests out of Manila, Elon decided to buy it from them. Elon is a good businessman and he has done very well for himself. He and his wife Sylvia chose to live and raise their family in the Philippines and they continue to live there to this day. He finally retired a few years ago, but the company is still being managed by his family.

The United States

The rest of us came to the United States and stayed here: Our oldest brother Robert paved the way. After getting his Ph.D. in marine biology from the University of Washington, he made his life in the Seattle area. Robert was the most generous person I knew. He was always sharing whatever he had, leaving care packages of food on our front door. He passed away in 2004, at only 72 years old.

My younger sister Eileen graduated at the very top of her high school class of 200, which was very impressive. She was always a very smart student. She was admitted to the National Taiwan University without even having to take an entrance exam, a university known for having the most difficult exam. But she wanted to come to the U.S. She earned a Ph.D. in mathematics from the University of Washington and had a long teaching career, first at the University of California, and then as head of the computer science and mathematics department at Menlo College. She even received the 1985 faculty award there. She still lives in California with her husband. They had two children, a daughter who lives in New York and a son who is a concert cellist with the Freemont Orchestra. She is a grandmother now, too, and really helped take care of her grandchildren when they were little, just like she did with my girls. Eileen is sincere and calm, and she does everything with her heart.

My younger brother, Lee, went to school at the University of Washington and earned a degree in aeronautical engineering. He worked at Boeing for over 40 years, first helping to develop the 737 airplane and then went to China as part of the Boeing salesforce. After the Second World War, when the Communist Party defeated the Nationalist government, the relationship between China and the U.S. was severed. President Nixon's visit to China in 1972 greatly improved relations between the two countries, and not long after that, China started to do business with Boeing. In an ironic twist of fate, Lee was sent there as part of his job. Life is really funny like that sometimes. Lee's wife is originally from Germany and they live in a big, beautiful house on the outskirts of Seattle. They raised two sons and did such a great job taking care of those boys. Lee was a really good dad. He has a lot of health problems, but he has been always been a strong-minded person, so he survived. He uses a wheeled walker and has a car with special features to help him get around and take care of daily needs. He even still does some yard work. His life isn't easy right now, but you would never know how much pain and suffering he's going through. He's always so cheerful and has such a good attitude.

My younger siblings did not have as much of the Japanese education that Robert and I did. By the time they were old enough to remember very much, the Japanese occupation was over. They don't remember as much as we do about the time before the war, about having to always be perfect. Their childhood was very different. But all of my siblings are really impressive to me. Each of them did such a wonderful job getting a great education and building great careers. I know my parents must have been proud.

Three of my siblings, from left: Elon, Eileen, and Lee.

The Philippines

During the mid-1970s, when I realized how busy I was going to be visiting my parents in Manila and taking care of their house in Taiwan, I decided to take early retirement from Boeing Computer Services, where I had been working as a systems analyst.

My father's health started to decline even more, and regrettably he passed away on July 26, 1987. He was 83 years old, and my parents had been married for over 60 years.

My mother was not quite happy staying with my brother and really wanted to go back to Taiwan so she could be near her sisters and friends. We knew she could not be alone there, and none of us could stay with her for long periods of time, so I started taking her back and forth from the Philippines to Taiwan for short stays. A few years later, when she got sick, too, we got together and decided it would be best to move her back, full time, to the Philippines. Her health insurance benefits were in Taiwan, the Philippines is close enough that she could get back if she needed medical care, and Elon could take care of her daily needs. It was the easiest and best thing for her.

On one of the trips, when I was taking her back to my brother's house in Manila from Taiwan, we ran into a big problem. Her visa kept getting delayed because our family had not paid the Taiwan estate taxes due on my father's estate. In Taiwan, estate taxes are due upon a person's death, and somehow in all the shuffling around, we had forgotten to take care of that. So, I hired a caretaker for a short time to take care of my mother, so I could gather all the necessary documents to calculate the amount of tax owed and pull together the funds to pay it. It was such a monumental task for me that I lost about 5 pounds. But my mother was elated, because it all meant that she got to stay in Taiwan for a little longer. Joe realized that I needed some help, so he took a few weeks off from work to flew to Taiwan to help me.

My father had a lot of stocks. Not only did he have stock in the Formosa Plastics Company founded by Mr. Y.C. Wang, but he also been investing for years in a cookware company called Datong. At that time, stocks were all still on actual pieces of paper, nothing was digital, and all of those paper stocks were sitting in a bank in Taipei. So, I went to the bank to go withdraw enough stock certificates out of my safety deposit box to pay the tax, which turned out to be quite a large amount. Not only did I have to get possession of the stock certificates, but the bank had to stamp each individual piece of paper for them to be considered endorsed. I sat there for what seemed like forever—stamp, stamp, stamp—waiting for them to finish. Then Joe and I put all of them into four big, brown bags and took them to the government offices to pay the taxes. It was pouring down rain as Joe and I walked the streets and rode the buses of Taipei, all the while carrying four bags full of stocks that had been officially stamped by the bank, so they were basically like cash at that point. It was so much money! I could have been robbed, lost them, or dropped them all in the rain. Luckily for me, none of that happened and I made it to the tax office, where I then had to get each individual stock stamped as received by them, and get the paid receipt for my dad's estate, so Mother could finally get her visa and go back to the Philippines.

I did it but Mother was not happy about it. I felt bad that I could not accommodate one of her last wishes, after all she had done for me in my life, but it was best that Elon take care of her.

About three years later, my mother also passed away. She was 86 years old. Both of my parents' ashes are still in the Philippines, being stored in a Catholic church. Even though I haven't figured out all of the details yet, someday I am going to get their ashes back to their home, back to Taiwan, where all of their family's ashes and tombs are, where they spent their lives. They should be in Taiwan.

During that whole time my parents were sick and living with my brother, Joe and I would go back to the hot springs every year and take care of the house. You never know what can happen to a house when it is sitting empty; besides, all of their belongings were still there. Everything was there from all of the years—my grandmother's wedding dress, family pictures, everything from the war. Maintaining the house was kind of expensive, but I felt it was worth it to keep all of our family's treasures.

Over the years, my father's longtime chauffeur had become very wealthy. With the help of my father, he also purchased a lot of stock in the Formosa Plastics Company, and later took that money and invested it in a construction company. He suggested to us that we hire him to build a duplex where my parents' house had stood and give him one of the units as part of the construction cost. We agreed. So, he tore down the old house and built a big, beautiful duplex on the same lot. The house he built is beautiful. He obviously knew a lot about construction and was good at that business.

After my mother passed away, Joe and I stayed in the house when we went to Taiwan to take care of financial matters and we hired workers to do various maintenance projects on the house. I have many wonderful memories of inviting my aunts and other relatives and friends to come over and enjoy the place once again. Several years later, my siblings and I got together to discuss what to do with the house.

The rebuilt house in Shin Pei Tou, Taiwan.

We took a vote and the majority decision was to sell the house and move the most important items to Elon's. My sister and I took some of the remaining items, so those things are preserved.

China

We all inherited some land and some money from my father, but we also inherited stocks from the Formosa Plastic Corporation where Father worked as the CEO for so many years. In 2018, the company was ranked as the world's sixth-largest chemical company in sales. That same year *Forbes* ranked the company as No. 758 on its list of the world's largest public companies. The company was built in the 1950s to produce plastic material, and it was amazing to me that it had continued such impressive success for such a long time. The president of the company, Wang Yung-ching, was forever thankful to my father for helping him secure those additional funds from a U.S. bank to expand his company. It made a difference in the company's success for years to come.

After we inherited all of those stocks from our father, I learned how to be a stock trader. I never loved it, though. In fact, I find stocks to be stressful. I don't mean to sound ungrateful; I am very grateful for all of the sacrifices of my parents and everything they left us. They didn't just spend everything they made; they left an inheritance for all of us. I want to be able to do the same, to pass something on to my children and grandchildren, and stock trading always feels so risky. You never knew if stocks were going to go up or if they were going to go down. So, I came up with a strategy that helped me feel more comfortable with the level of risk. I took any cash dividends I received and I put those in the bank, but the stock dividends I let accumulate. That's how I ended up with so much stock! I never touched the dividends! The rest of it, I treated sort of like a game. I called the broker (I had enough shares so they would take my call) and said if it goes up this amount, then sell this many shares, and things like that. Then, I didn't spend the profit, I just let it sit in the account and used it to pay the taxes. So it was like a game, the money almost did not seem real.

Using this strategy, playing this little game, the original shares that my father left for me eventually accumulated to over one million shares. Each share was only worth about $2 to $3 USD, but when I sold 20,000 or 30,000 shares at a time, and did that often, it became a good sum. I had a lot of fun during this time working with the stockbroker. She was making a good commission off of me, so she was very helpful. In general, an investment broker would probably tell you that you should not put all your money into just one stock, but I didn't know the stock market in Taiwan, and I only had one stock to play with.

I kept the stock in Taiwan as long as I could, rather than selling them and transferring the funds to the U.S. I was so emotionally connected to the Formosa Plastic Corporation and those stocks that I didn't want to let them go. Father always treasured the family things and preserved them so well. That is the reason I ignored the idea of diversifying and trying to make it a better investment. Luckily, it turned out to be a great investment. And since I also have citizenship in Taiwan, I just translated the Taiwan income tax return into English and filed my return with the IRS.

Although I had been gradually selling my Taiwan stocks for several years, I got some advice from my attorney that I needed to start simplifying my life, principally to not be a burden to my family after I'm gone. Fortunately, during my 18 years of ownership, the Formosa company continued to prosper under great management, earning me a good deal of money, but I heeded my attorney's advice and completely sold all of my stocks in 2018, transferred the funds to the U.S., and closed all my bank accounts in Taiwan in 2019. I used some of the money to invest, and the rest I divided up into an Opportunity Trust for my descendants. If they want to start a business or go to school, there are restrictions on how they can use it, but it is there for the next 100 years. I set it up for that length of time because I want it to last, not just be used up in one or two generations. I would also like to add in the Opportunity Trust that if one uses funds from it, he or she has to make the best effort to put some funds back.

With something set aside for my children and their children, I then used some of the funds from the stock sale to invest in the future of education in China. Education was always so important to my parents. They made sure that each of us children had an opportunity to get the best education possible, even if that meant sending us to another country to get it. Repaying gratitude was also very important to my father. In fact, it was so important to my father that he repay his gratitude toward his older brothers for sending him to a top business university in Japan that, at one point when I was a young teenager, he let several of his brothers' children live with us so they could attend higher-rated schools in Taipei. We provided them with food, and housing, and my mother even tutored them in the evenings to help them get better grades. So, I am grateful for what my parents did for me, and following their example, I thought it was only right that their money is used to help further the education of other children. So, in 2010, I started a scholarship program for children in small farming villages, where people are in the greatest need.

The program was started with the help of my Chinese friend, Mr. Chi Wong. Mr. Wong had already established his own charity foundation and was instrumental in coordinating with his contacts already in China to help us identify schools and children who would most benefit from our donation.

My scholarships are not merely merit-based. A student's grade-point average is considered, but it is of secondary importance. I am much more interested in understanding their family conditions. I ask questions on the application about where they live, whom they live with, what they do after school, and how much time they have to study. Some of these kids are taking care of sick grandparents, doing housework, or working to help pay for tuition or even food, and that greatly affects their ability to do well in school. So, family conditions are an important factor in choosing whom we sponsor. The money we donate is called a scholarship, but it is not for the tuition. It is used to buy books, shoes, clothing, or even living expenses, whatever is needed to help the child attend school.

I didn't want to just give money blindly, either, not knowing where it was going. I wanted to meet the students, actually put the money in their hand and see their faces when they realized they wouldn't have to worry so much. So, a few years ago Mr. Wong arranged two separate trips for Joe and me to go to visit the southern provinces of Guangxi 廣西 and Yunnan 雲南 to meet the students I'd been sponsoring. The school in Yunnan was located in a village that sat on top of a 6,500-foot mountain, and it took two drivers and seven hours of driving along a winding scenic road to get there. But it was worth it, because when I arrived, I got to sit down with them in the classroom, and eat lunch with them. All of the students, and even the principals, wrote letters to thank us, and they told us how much we had helped improve their lives.

Many of my Taiwanese friends wonder why I chose China, instead of the U.S. or Japan, or even Taiwan as the place to donate the money. But China is the poorest of them all and has the greatest need. A mere $500 scholarship will greatly help the life of a child in a small village there.

None of my close friends from Taiwan came to the U.S. for college; their parents could not afford it. Many of them have never been to China, either, so they just don't know how great the need is in the world. My brothers and sister and I were very lucky. We've seen, learned, and experienced things very few people from our particular kind of background have.

But when I go home, I am still the same. Some people grow older, grow apart, and forget their friends, but I try to stay connected with my past and all the people from it. No matter how much any of us change, we are still friends, we are still together, just like the Japanese culture that shaped us so long ago.

In the fall of 2019, when I attended the reunions of both grade school in Japan and the middle school in Taiwan, most of the classmates said that they would like to make it the last reunion as we are close to the late 80s and some of us were beginning to have health problems. I was the only one who attended from overseas, and Joe had been coming with me for so many years that my classmates treated him like one of our own. Some of them said to me that if we wanted to continue to come back, some of them would like to continue to get together. So, I determined that we would go back as long as Joe and I were in good enough health to make the trip.

The principal and dean of the grade school to which I donated the scholarship.

Chinese grade school students.

Going to lunch with the grade school students.

All these years I have been going to Taiwan and to Japan and staying in the same hotels. I have gotten well acquainted with some of the employees and even some of the guests who also stay in the same hotels year after year. They became my good friends and to this day I still stay in contact with ex-employees and friends that I've made through the years, and we get together whenever we are in Japan or Taiwan.

I have already booked my trip for my next class reunion. In fact, as soon as one is over, I start booking the trip for the next one. It's not cheap. Japan is an expensive place. But going back for the reunion is important, even if costly, and I will continue to go for as long as I can.

MEXICO

AFTER I RETIRED FROM Boeing, while Joe was still running the wine-making store, we really started to travel a lot. I enjoy organizing our trips myself, rather than going through a travel agency, and that has, at times, led us on some pretty interesting adventures. It also saved us a lot of money, and after I stopped working, that seemed to be even more important.

We visited just about all the major cities in China, Japan, and Taiwan, but one of the most unforgettable trips was to Jiuzhaigou (九寨溝, Valley of Nine Fortified Villages) in the Sichuan Province of China. We went not long after the village was discovered and just after it was officially opened to tourism in 1987. The scenery was incredible: the multi-level waterfalls, the crystal waters, and the colorful lakes. It was even inscribed by UNESCO in 1992 as a World Heritage Site.

Over the years, I've found quite a few ways to make travel more affordable. One of the most important things I learned is that it's much more cost-effective to book international travel from overseas, not from within the U.S. For example, when traveling in China, I would book trips with the travel agencies that were operating inside the hotel lobby where we were staying, and I usually selected a tour group with an English speaking guide for Joe. That is how we ended up making a trip to Mongolia.

Cascading clear blue water at Jiuzhaigou.

A tree under the clear water at Jiuzhaigou.

Joe and I in Jiuzhaigou.

Tibetan Village scene at Jiuzhaigou.

Joe on a camel in Mongolia.

Yurt of Gher, where we stayed the night in Mongolia.

In 2006, we flew from Beijing, China, to Ulaanbaatar, the capital of Mongolia, where we met up with a tour guide and a driver who took us on a one week trip through the Gobi Desert. We drove every day and camped every night in a yurt. At each campsite, we had a chance to talk with the other tourists and I was surprised to meet so many people from all around the world who had come to visit the Gobi Desert. I was also surprised to learn that the Gobi Desert was not all sand, but rather a vast gravel desert with no roads or even tracks to follow. The driver just kept driving out across the gravel and I was amazed at how he knew which direction to go.

After many years of traveling around, getting acquainted with the different histories and cultures of the world, we finally made our first trip to Mexico to visit Merida in Yucatan, Guadalajara in Jalisco, and Mexico City.

The most memorable part was our visit to the National Museum of Anthropology in Mexico City. The museum contains significant archaeological and anthropological artifacts from Mexico's

An iguana on a tree in downtown Puerto Vallarta.

Joe's pride in fishing.

pre-Columbian heritage. Pre-Columbian art refers to the visual arts of indigenous people of the Caribbean and North, Central, and South America. It was so exciting to spend a whole day getting to learn the history and see the exquisite stonework, such as the Stone of the Sun (the Aztec calendar stone) and the Aztec Xochipilli statue.

Although we had traveled extensively at that point, Mexico was not like any place Joe and I had been before. Everywhere I looked I saw birds, animals, and flowers. The food was so fresh and most of all, I loved the music. Even the sad songs they sing made me feel cheery because the melodies are so beautiful.

We had heard that Puerto Vallarta was where the Hollywood director, John Houston, made the film *The Night of the Iguana* starring Richard Burton and Ava Gardner and that Richard Burton and Elizabeth Taylor had bought a house and were living there. But prior to the filming of *The Night of the Iguana*, I had heard that a lot of Canadians were spending the winter months in Puerto Vallarta, and as it continued to gain popularity, regular people came to realize that it wasn't just a place for the rich and famous but also an affordable place to travel and enjoy beautiful beaches, food, and the fantastic winter weather on the western coast of Mexico. Joe and I decided we wanted to go there, too. So, in 1982, we booked our trip and rented a little house, which was owned by a British-American from Seattle, located 2.6 miles north of Puerto Vallarta in the small town called Aramara.

We were surprised to see how small the downtown area of Puerta Vallarta was. There was a narrow strip of the boardwalk called the Malecon, which runs along the waterfront, but there were not many businesses or stores in that area.

While we were walking along the Malecon, we saw an American real estate agent standing in front of a real estate office. I was glad that I was able to ask him some questions in English about the town, and being in real estate myself, I was also anxious to see if he would show us a typical Mexican house. He agreed to show us one that was owned by an older Canadian couple who were moving back to Canada to take care of the man's poor health, but the agent said they were asking too high of a price.

Puerto Vallarta, Malecon Boardwalk.

When we arrived at the house, the wife was heading out, but we had a chance to meet the man. We were introduced to the owner, Mr. Bogdan Koscec, who admitted to us that he did not really want to sell the house. He was Croatian, had immigrated to Canada from Yugoslavia, then he and his wife had bought a home in Mexico. His health had started to deteriorate, so his wife wanted to take him back to Canada for better medical treatment. But he liked Puerto Vallarta so much that he said he would rather stay there and die.

As we continued talking with Mr. Koscec, he began to share some of his experiences during the Second World War in Europe, so I shared my war experience in Asia with him. We got so involved in exchanging our stories of the war that Joe and I almost forgot to see the house. The agent was very patient with us but we decided to not take more of his time, so the owner quickly showed us around and then we left. Afterward, Joe and I both realized that although we had talked to the man a lot, we hadn't actually gotten to see the house very well.

We were scheduled to return to Seattle the next afternoon, so we went back to town and in the morning went over to the Malecon area to have another look around. When I looked up the hill, I tried to remember how to get up to Mr. Koscec's house. We started walking up the hill, just to see how far it was. Surprisingly, Mrs. Koscec was looking out the glass door and as she saw us approaching, she began to strongly gesture with her hands, inviting us to come in. This time they showed us all around the house and told us about everything they were doing to maintain the place.

It was a very small house, only about 20 feet wide and 30 feet long. As you entered, you could walk on the left side straight back to a small bedroom and bathroom, but on the right side was a stairway leading to the second floor where there was a small area with a living room and dining room combined and a terrace with a beautiful view of the ocean. The kitchen and the bathroom were in the front part of the house, where there was a small balcony overlooking the street. The name of the house was Casa El Balcon (Spanish for "The Balcony House"), and the name remains the same today.

We left the house that day and headed straight to the airport to catch our plane home. We were not actually considering buying a house in Mexico. It was our very first time visiting Puerta Vallarta, but we learned so much about the town and the house from Mr. and Mrs. Koscec. As we sat down in our seats in the plane and started to get comfortable, Joe turned to me and out of the blue said, "Joyce, I think I would like to buy a house here."

I couldn't believe my ears. We had only looked at that house because I'm a real estate investor and was simply curious. "That's a terrible idea," I said. "Banks won't even loan money for property here because it's not a good place to invest. It's too much of a risk."

But Joe just looked at me and said, "Sometimes, Joyce, you should do something just because you like it, not because it makes good sense."

As the plane took off, I started thinking about what Joe said. I knew he was right. We had both really loved Puerto Vallarta. So, without any further hesitation, we went back home, figured out a plan to come up with the cash, and made them an offer for $82,000. Even though that was below their asking price, they accepted it without even making a counteroffer.

Only about three weeks later, we again sat down with Teadore (Ted) Koscec and his wife, Bozena, across the same little patio table on the terrace with a beautiful view of the ocean, and signed the paperwork on the sale. Joe and I were now homeowners in Puerta Vallarta, Mexico. It was at that moment that Bozena told us something she hadn't mentioned before. She said that the night before we came to look at the house, she had a dream that a Chinese lady with a white streak in her hair was going to buy her house. It was such a coincidence because at that time I had a streak of white hair just to the right of my forehead.

Like so many other things in my life, I guess buying that house was meant to be.

The house is in an area called Colonia el Cerro (Hill Suburb), three blocks up a very steep hill from the Malecon Boardwalk. The streets are so narrow that only one car can pass, as cars are usually parked along one side. From inside the houses, you can hear the street vendors calling out with food, vegetables, shoe repair and knife sharpening services, and the like. Some of our Mexican neighbors often play very loud music, even into the wee hours of the night. One neighbor across the street would sometimes play his music until 2 or 3 o'clock in the morning, but I did not complain. He came home from work every day around midnight after working long hours in a restaurant, and he liked to listen to music to relax. I was learning about the culture of the people who lived around me, of my new neighbors.

As I started to interact more and more with Mexican people, I decided to change my first name because so many of them mispronounced my name or were not sure how to pronounce it. In Spanish, the "J" is pronounced as an "H" so Joyce sounded more like Hoyce. Alegria means joy, similar to Joyce, so that's what I chose.

It turned out that there were many Americans and other English-speaking people who lived in our neighborhood as well, and they liked to have parties. As we came here more and more often, and met more people, Joe and I started getting more and more invitations

Pulitzer-winning author Allen Drury on a visit to the Miramar House.

to those parties. So, we went. Sometimes there would be 90 or 100 people on the rooftops, too many to really get to know, but we were able to foster a few close relationships.

One neighbor in a condo a few doors down really liked to cook, so he threw dinner parties quite often and we were usually on the list. He also had a big van, so at some point in the night he would often invite anyone who wanted to join to pile into his van for a drive around the countryside visiting interesting places. One of the party regulars was a blind man, but he knew the area better than any of us, so he always ended up giving directions.

At the time, Puerto Vallarta was still a trendy place, and we sometimes found ourselves rubbing elbows with rich and famous people. One time, we were at a party at the house of some famous fashion model, and we met the Pulitzer Prize-winning author Allen Drury. His novel *Advise and Consent* not only earned him a Pulitzer Prize, but was eventually made into a movie. He was an interesting man and I enjoyed talking with him. He said to me, "Joyce, you should think about writing your life story," but at that time writing my life story was far from my mind.

Miramar House (Casa el Balcon)

After several years, we decided to remodel the house and make it a place where we could start spending a lot more time. There was a yard in the back, which demanded a lot of upkeep, so the first thing we wanted to do was extend the house to the back, adding usable square footage and getting rid of the yard. In Seattle, I had a lot of contacts; I knew exactly whom to call for any type of work that I needed to have done. I did not know anyone in Mexico, and I was nervous about hiring contractors in another country, especially one where I wasn't even fluent in the language yet.

Then, one day I met my neighbor, Beverly. Beverly was a feisty lady who loved to walk up into the woods to pick orchids. She always carried a gun with her, for protection. She seemed like a woman who knew how to take care of herself. She had also done a lot of work to her house. I had finally found someone who could give me advice on regulations and recommendations for whom to hire. I was so grateful for Beverly, and really leaned on her a lot early on, before my Spanish was up to par.

We later found out that our friend Beverly was none other than Beverly Harrel, owner of the famed Cottontail Ranch brothel just outside of Las Vegas. She invited us several times to come see her in Vegas, but I did not want to go. I knew her as my friend Beverly from The Hill, and I wanted to keep it that way.

A few years later, as I was reading the section in the Seattle Sunday newspaper, which listed the passing of well-known celebrities, I saw the name "Beverly Harrell." I turned my head away from the newspaper because I didn't want to know it could be the same Beverly that I knew. Then I found out it was, in fact, the same Beverly.

Puerto Vallarta sits on a big bay and our house is in about the center of the bay high up on a hill, overlooking the bay on one side and with a view of the mountains from the other. The street it sits on is called Miramar. Mira means look and mar means ocean, so the street name can be translated to mean "see the ocean." The house is both ideally situated and named, and I was excited to turn it into a more suitable place for us.

Before I could hire Beverly's contractor to do the work, I had to hire an architect to design the new construction and to get the construction permits from the municipal office. I found someone local, and he designed for us a 3-story construction, since the width of the house is only about 6 meters. This would give us plenty of living space, but also not block the ocean view from the people who lived above us on the hill.

We rented a run-down little place a few blocks down the hill on Calle Arroyo, so that we could have a place to stay while our house was under construction. There was no roof on the terrace and it had a terrible shower, but it was owned by an American lady, so we could easily communicate with her. It was also really close to our house, so we could easily walk over and check on construction every day.

Joe was still going back and forth to Seattle to check on the wine shop, but I stayed in Mexico to oversee the work, with intermittent short trips to Taiwan to take care of financial matters and to see my parents. The local architect we had hired only came to check on the job once in a while, which left me to work directly with the contractors and the workers. During one of my trips to Taiwan, Joe took over my job of overseeing the construction. His Spanish wasn't as good as mine was, and wasn't really sufficient for good communication with the workers. When I returned from Taiwan, I found out that some of the jobs were not done correctly. That's when I decided to hire someone to help us correct the mistakes and finish the reconstruction project properly.

One day, I was at the bank taking care of another financial matter and I was explaining to my agent the difficult situation we

Our 3-story house on Miramar in Puerto Vallarta.

were having remodeling the house. I asked her if she knew someone, possibly one her clients, who could help me with the construction. I was so surprised, but before I could even finish talking, she gave me the name of an American architect-interior designer who had been working in Puerto Vallarta for many years. It was such a wonderful coincidence! This is how I met Walter Bauman, and that is when my luck finally changed.

Walter was such an incredible help to us. He took care of the house as though it was his own. He immediately talked to the contractor about everything that needed to be corrected, and then he moved on to helping me with the interior decorating and furniture selection. Since there were hardly any furniture stores in town, he drove five hours through the winding mountain road to Guadalajara to purchase the furniture from vendors he regularly did business with.

Meanwhile, Joe and I continued to monitor the workers as they finished the changes. We had done a lot of the remodeling work on our home and our rental properties in Seattle, but this was Mexico and I had to pay very close attention to even the smallest details. If you overpay a worker in Mexico, you usually don't get your money back, so it's critical that you get it right the first time.

It was a lot of work. For example, if you have a large order for materials, companies will deliver it to your house, but if you only need a few bags of cement or sand, or a small amount of bricks, you have to pick it up yourself. So, every time the contractor told me he needed additional materials, I drove our little car without air conditioning in the hot summer heat to pick it up. I just rolled down the windows and took a little towel to wrap around my neck to wipe the sweat. In the evenings, I had to take care of all the construction bookkeeping and notes.

During all of this, I did my best to keep the socializing to a minimum, because Joe and I were just too busy. But Beverly lived just up the hill with her boyfriend and one evening they invited us for dinner. It had been a while since we'd gone out and we could use the break, so we accepted. It had been raining that day, but very lightly, so we carried our umbrellas with us as we walked up the hill. While we were eating dinner, it continued to rain heavier and heavier. A few short hours later, when we left for home, we were shocked to find that Arroyo Street, where our rent house was, was like a river. Matamoros Street, the one we had to cross to get home, was flooded halfway up our legs. I had never seen so much water, and it was running down those steep hills so fast that I was afraid that we would be swept away.

No one had been expecting a rainstorm. In fact, the roof wasn't even on our house yet! Luckily, we had stored our telephone and other electronics underneath the stairway for safekeeping, but I did not sleep a wink the whole night worrying. Before that night was over, we got 14 inches of rain. One house a few blocks away from us along with several adobe houses, which are made of sundried mud, clay, and straw, were totally demolished. But our house was miraculously okay.

When the construction was finally done, the house was so perfect and beautifully furnished. The views were gorgeous, and we could not thank Walter enough for what he had helped us create. We could hardly wait to invite our family and friends.

At first, though, we only went for short visits. Every time I got back home in Seattle, I would look in the mirror and notice how happy I looked. There was just something about my expression, and I knew it was because of spending time in Mexico. When you are surrounded by such beauty, your facial expression reflects it. And the people in Puerto Vallarta, both Mexicans and foreigners, most of the time greet each other with a smile and a friendly attitude even when just walking and passing each other on the street. So gradually we started staying longer and longer, until we were spending just over three months a year—January through the beginning of April, when the Seattle weather is rainy and cold.

We are so glad that we bought the house. Through the years, it has provided us, our daughters and their friends, my siblings and their families, and many others of our friends an opportunity to come to Mexico for the first time, to enjoy the beautiful town, and experience Mexican culture.

Quite often when people with cameras are up in our area looking for a place to take pictures, I will invite them to our house so they can capture the views from our balconies. Once, I saw four Japanese tourists walking through the intersection near our house, and one of them was carrying a large camera on his shoulder, so I invited them to come inside. I was excited to have the rare opportunity to speak to someone in Japanese and they were excited to see the views from our third floor. The symbolic sign of Puerto Vallarta is the Church of Our Lady of Guadalupe, known locally as La Iglesia de Nuestra Senora de Guadalupe, and it can be seen at a right angle diagonally from our back terrace. They were so delighted that the photographer just kept clicking and clicking his camera. In talking with them, I found out the two men were photographers from a Japanese tourism magazine called Tabi, which is the Japanese word for "Journey." They were with a writer and an actress, and they had all come on a cruise ship together and were taking pictures in town for an article they planned to publish about their trip.

A few months after they left, we received in the mail a *Tabi* magazine that they had published with the photos they took from our house, including one of Joe and me standing on the balcony. I did not know the actress very well, but when I went to Japan later, I showed her card to my friend there and she was so surprised that I met her. Her name is Fumi Dan, 壇ふみ, and she was nominated for the best supporting actress at the 17th Japanese Academy Prize. Her father is a novelist and she herself has won awards for her essays. I had no idea she was so well-known!

The wonderful view from the living room of Miramar house.

Our Lady of Guadalupe Cathedral, the view from the Miramar house.

Sunset views from the terrace of the Miramar house.

Second Construction - House on Iturbide Street

After several years, more and more Americans and other non-Mexicans started to move to the Hill neighborhood. There was an old apartment below our house that had been in disrepair for years and it started to become a real worry. If someone bought it, tore it down, and built something too tall in its place, it might obstruct the view from our house.

So, around the beginning of 2000, I started making an effort to meet the owner. We saw that he was starting to tear down the apartment. We know that In Puerto Vallarta, like any other city, there are construction laws and regulations, but if you have enough money to pay off the officials, you can sometimes bypass those laws and build whatever you want. I wanted to talk to him and try to find out what he was planning to build. But after several months, he suddenly stopped the construction. That was just as much of a concern, because in Puerto Vallarta, if an owner of the construction runs out of money, the unfinished eyesore might sit there for many years.

I found out the owner was Pepe Nuñez, and one day I saw him on the street and grabbed the opportunity to ask him why he had stopped construction. He said that the property owner below him was reconstructing a building that would block his view. I went home and started thinking. The property is 20 feet by 100 feet and sits on the slope. This might be our chance to protect our view.

Soon after that, I saw Pepe on the street again. This time I asked him if he would like to sell me his unfinished property. He asked me how much I would pay, but I told him I needed to put some thought into my answer and that I would get back to him the next day. I decided to make him an offer of $40,000 USD. I knew this was low, but I wanted to leave room for negotiation. Pepe was born and grew up in Puerto Vallarta when it was a small fishing village; he probably did not have any idea about property values in the area and was not familiar with real estate dealing, so he just threw at me the double price of $80,000. I accepted, but hesitantly.

In old Puerto Vallarta, I had been told that some people had just grabbed a piece of land and built a house on it, so the ownership was not always properly documented. I wanted to make sure Pepe had the proper documentation proving he was the real owner before I paid him any money, so I went to City Hall but what I found is that the documented map of the area was so old that it had not been updated in years. I decided to move forward with the process anyway, for fear that he would sell the property to someone else, so I made an appointment with a notary and explained to Pepe that he had to bring the ownership papers with him. I was so anxious leading up to the appointment, but as we were sitting down waiting to see the notary, I saw to my great relief that the document in his hand had the names of both him and his mother. Another moment of tension occurred, though, when the notary told Pepe that he had to pay capital gains taxes in the amount of $7,000 USD. Pepe's face went blank when he heard the figure, because he did not know how much that would be in pesos. To close the deal, I decided to offer to pay his capital gains costs, which he happily accepted, and we were able to finalize the sale that day.

We sat on the property for a while, trying to decide what we wanted to do with it. We couldn't figure out whether to tear the building down and make it into a green space, since we saw fewer and fewer iguanas and lizards in the area, or to build another house. We finally decided to build another house for my daughters and grandchildren to be able to enjoy beautiful Puerto Vallarta for years to come. Besides, this time around we would know whom to call.

I hired the son of the first architect who had worked on the Miramar house and I asked Walter to work with the architect on the design. The maximum height allowed was three stories, but to protect mine and my neighbors' views from the Miramar house, I purposely requested a two-story building. They came up with the two-story house, configured into an upper and lower duplex, with each three-bedroom unit being about 2,000 square feet. Then, one of my neighbors introduced me to a good contractor and he brought with him an assistant and 15 additional

The duplex house on Iturbide in Puerto Vallarta.

workers. At the height of the construction, there were sometimes as many as 25 workers, so they were an efficient crew.

I went to the job site every day and I noticed during their lunch break that a lot of the men hardly had any food to eat. A few had one or two tomatoes or some bananas in their hat. Some had nothing to eat and were just sitting down talking. It is a Chinese custom that the owner provides food for the workers; besides, I wanted the workers to have enough energy to do a good job, so I decided to start feeding them lunch every day. At first, I went to the store and bought prepared Mexican dishes, then I decided to make them Chinese Ham Bao, which are steamed buns filled with pork. They all seemed to like them a lot, and I got pretty good at making them, so I started giving some to my neighbors, also. They became quite a hit! Some of my neighbors still ask about them many years later, and tell me they would happily take some if I ever make them again.

Things had been going well on the job for several months, but as the construction progressed, I started to notice some of the workers stopped showing up. So, when the contractor went on vacation, I asked the subcontractor why fewer and fewer men were on the job. He pulled me to the side and told me secretly that the contractor had not been paying some people the amount they were supposed to get. I had given the contractor money up front to pay his men, and he was supposed to distribute the payments, so I had reason to suspect that he had taken the money for his own use. There was also another incident that gave me even more concern. Several weeks earlier, he had given me a receipt for five loads of bricks, but I found out from the deliveryman that we only purchased four loads, so he must have pocketed the extra money.

So, while the contractor was still on his vacation, I talked to the subcontractor about taking over the job and he agreed. Now, I just had to tell the contractor that he was fired. I was a little nervous, and people warned me that it might be bad, but I had taken care of lunch for them and had tried my best to be thoughtful every day, so I hoped it would be okay. I gave a lot of careful thought to how I was going to tell him, but even still he got very upset when he learned about my decision to replace him with his subcontractor. I believe in being humane, so I offered him good severance pay and he reluctantly accepted. The subcontractor took over the job and, with Walter's help, they were able to finish the job in about nine months. On the very last day of construction, I decided to hire a Mariachi band and provide food and drinks and give them a big thank you fiesta. It was such a great party and all of us had a great time.

After the house was built, Walter took Joe and me out-of-town furniture shopping again. He knew exactly what furniture we needed to go to where in the house, and it was so much fun going to all the different furniture stores and secondhand shops. Whatever Walter said, I just accepted and wrote the checks. Everything is perfect. All the furniture, paintings, wall decorations, lamps, and console tables all beautifully fit.

After so many projects together, Walter became not only our designer, but also a good friend. We continued to keep in touch afterward and always got together whenever Joe and I were in Puerto Vallarta. A few years later, when we called to check in on him, his partner told us that Walter was severely sick with liver cancer and in the hospital, so we flew straight to Ajijic to visit him. As we stood there next to his bed, he was still asking me about the house and was telling me how I should take care of the house. His soul was so completely tied to home decorating that he was talking about it even on his death bed. We just held his hands and tried to control the tears coming down.

Enjoying Spending Time in Mexico

It has been almost 40 years since that first visit to Mexico in 1982, and quite a lot has happened since then. I tried my best to learn Spanish and to continue to become more and more fluent so that I would be able to interact better with people. I also subscribed to the local Spanish newspaper and became familiar with what was happening in town and in the country. If I don't understand some of the articles or if I have questions, I just ask my housekeeper. She is in her 40s, single, and seems to be keeping up with the current news. We are so thankful to have had such a devoted housekeeper and a maintenance man who lived close by and helped us take care of both houses when we are away.

Even though Joe and I went through the two construction projects, I made most of the decisions and ended up dealing with the management and the maintenance afterward. Some of those experiences were very challenging for me, but others were extremely pleasant, and I learned a lot in my dealings with the workers and the Mexican government. Looking back, I feel it was those life experiences that helped me to understand and appreciate the Mexican people and their culture better. After so many years of interacting with them, I am very comfortable with conversations in Spanish. When I hear traditional Mexican music, I understand the lyrics, and I think that helps me better understand the heart of the Mexican people.

This is the fourth phase of my life. In each phase, I learned the language and steeped myself in the culture, and have been greatly enriched by it. For each phase—Japanese, Chinese, American, and Mexican—I still enjoy listening to the music and recalling the time I have lived in each one.

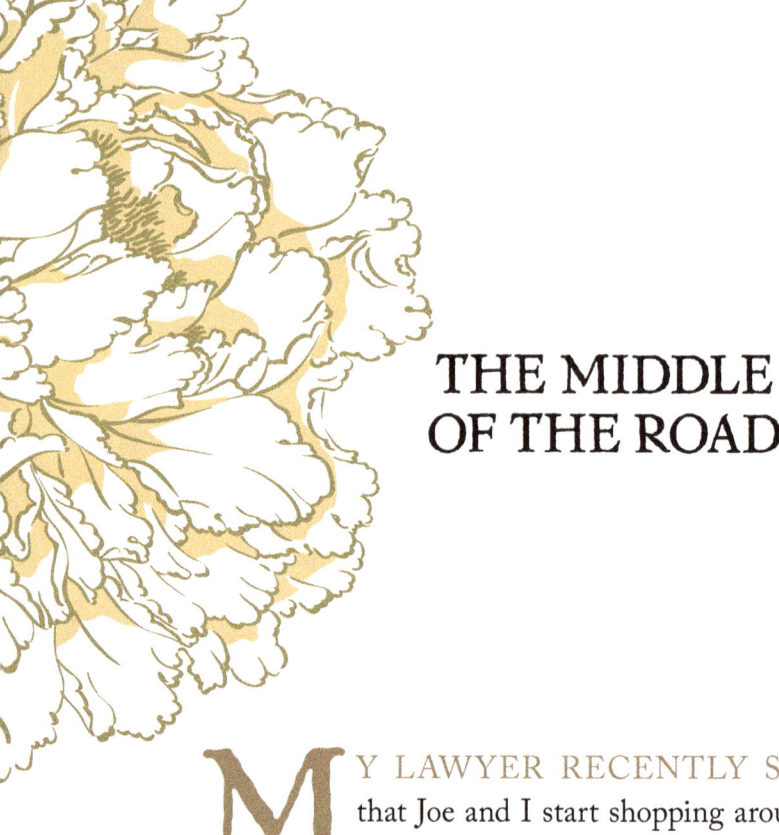

THE MIDDLE OF THE ROAD

MY LAWYER RECENTLY SUGGESTED that Joe and I start shopping around for a senior living center.

"We aren't ready for that yet!" I told him. "We are still healthy. We still want to travel."

"You have to make those choices for yourself before it's too late," he told me. "Otherwise, someone else will end up making the choices for you."

So, we looked around at a few places. They were really nice, and of course we were treated very well while touring all of them. They showed us the rooms, the living spaces and the gardens, and they invited us to stay and have lunch. But I don't eat the kind of food they serve there, like pizza and hamburgers, and I saw so many people who were already in wheelchairs or suffering from dementia that it made me depressed. Besides, they were very expensive. I thought if I had to live there, I would get old really fast.

So, I told Joe that we should just stay right there in our Seattle house for as long as we want to. We installed the tram that goes up the hill from the house to the garage years ago, so we can use that to haul groceries, or even to ride if our mobility decreases. And if we eventually need more help, we can have a caretaker move into the basement apartment. That will cost less than paying for a senior care center, and we get to live in our own house. But I don't plan on any of that happening any time soon.

In fact, that's when I decided to hire a trainer. We are investing in our health, not in a senior care center. Whether we are in Seattle or Puerta Vallarta, we go to the gym and work with a trainer three days a week. And we eat healthy, too, and try to drink plenty of water, especially first thing in the morning on an empty stomach. Water helps to detox the body and starts each day with a clean slate. My father died from colon cancer, so I know I have to watch that kind of thing.

I asked my trainer what they eat to keep up with their strength training and he said a lot of carbohydrates, but that's too extreme for me. Joe and I prefer to have our big meal of the day around 2 or 3 o'clock in the afternoon, then by the time we go to bed that night, most of the food has digested and we don't go to bed feeling full and heavy. If we get really hungry late in the evening, we just have a few crackers or something. We sleep better that way, and it works really well for us.

A few years ago, I met a man at the bus stop in Japan. I saw him walking up there, kind of slowly, so I paid attention. When he made it to the stop, I struck up a conversation, and I asked him how old he was. He told me that he was 97 years old. I was so impressed that a man of his age was still walking around the city, still taking the bus. Out of curiosity, I asked him what he ate every day. "I have eaten natto every single day for most of my life," he said.

Natto is a fermented soybean that is typically eaten as a breakfast food, sometimes served with mustard or soy sauce. I know that Japanese people live longer than anyone else. *Maybe it's the natto*, I thought. It smells kind of strong, and it's a little sticky. I had been eating it a few times a week before that, but I've been eating it every day since then.

Another thing I do is I try to forgive. Forgiveness is actually a selfish act, another way of taking good care of yourself. When I'm managing my different business enterprises, if a worker doesn't do a good job for me or I end up losing money because someone wasn't paying attention,

I don't cut that person off. I might be able to utilize them for something else later, or maybe that person knows someone who might be able to help me in another way. Even though they did a bad thing, I don't shut the door on them completely. Holding grudges is really not good for you, so I try not to hang on to unpleasantness from other people. I just let it go, forget it. Besides, you never know what other people are going through.

I want to be around for a long time to come. As long as Joe and I stay physically and mentally fit, we still have a lot of things we want to do. I want to do some more real estate investing while I can still manage everything myself. I don't want to leave behind a burden of properties for my children, but I enjoy real estate and would like to buy one or two more properties.

And I've always wanted to take dance lessons, but never had the time. Now we do! Joe and I first met at a dance club, and we still enjoy dancing together. We don't know any fancy steps, we just dance according to the music, but people often comment about how well we dance together. It's good exercise, too.

I would also like to take some more computer classes. It's interesting to me to solve problems like that and I would like to get more familiar with programs people use now, because it changes all the time.

I want to go to parts of the U.S. that we've never been to, and I would like to visit Vietnam. I was so impressed with the Vietnamese refugees that I met who had come to the U.S. after the war. They came here and started businesses and became independent contributing citizens right away; that impressed me about their people and culture. I would like to see the country they came from.

And I want to continue going to Taiwan to attend my yearly middle school reunion and to visit my aunts and cousins who are still alive there. Joe and I always stay in the same hotel when we go; we get the same room and everything. A lot of Japanese people stay in that hotel, because it's reasonable, so I get to meet a lot of Japanese tourists. Since the Taiwanese clerks do not always speak fluent Japanese, I find myself translating for them a lot, giving them advice like a tour guide.

Joe and I dancing during the celebration of our granddaughter Erica's wedding.

Sometimes I almost feel like I'm working there, but I enjoy it because I get to meet so many people and often end up becoming good friends with them. I now correspond with several people that I've met that way.

I enjoy getting to know people everywhere I go. At the gym, at the grocery store, or any place that we go regularly. I don't let mine or anyone else's station in life determine whom I'm friends with, and my friends are friends forever. It's kind of nice, having friends everywhere.

No matter where we are, we like to find a few good restaurants and go to those same places over and over again. We get to know the owner, become friends, and sometimes they even give us discounts. There is a Japanese restaurant in Seattle called Maneki where we've been going for 34 years. Maneki means invite or beckon in Japanese and refers to the century-old tradition of the Maneki-neko or beckoning cat, which are the little cat dolls that you usually see in the front window or by the cash register in Asian restaurants. When we are in Seattle, we go to Maneki every Friday night at 5:30, and we sit in the same spot. They make really good sushi rolls, but when we first started going I used to special order the rolls just the way I liked—scallops, avocado, cucumber, shrimp, and mayonnaise, with a crunch on the outside. Once, I even drew a little picture for the chef, so they would know exactly how I wanted it made; they put my picture up on the wall so they would remember. That became my regular order, and the chefs started calling it the JoJo roll. One day, I heard a man a few tables away order a JoJo roll, too. I thought maybe I had misheard him, but then I looked and saw that my JoJo roll was officially on the menu! Joe and I got a real kick out of that.

You know, you think when you first get married that your married life is going to be better, better, better. But, that's not really how it is. In fact, some things get worse, and you have to learn how to adjust. It is the little things like someone not making the bed the right way or getting coffee grounds on the kitchen counter, that can really affect a marriage. But even after more than 60 years Joe and I still laugh together, and we still like doing a lot of the same things together. We also share the housework, and I think that kind of thing helps keep us together, too.

He has his own responsibilities and I have mine. I cook and he does the dishes. I drive when we are in Seattle, because he drives too slowly, and he drives when we are in Mexico, because traffic in Puerto Vallarta is not very busy and I am not good with directions. We still go to the same restaurants and enjoy the same things we have for over 60 years. These are the things that keep people together for a long time.

After so many years of observing family life, I have learned a few things. If I were to give a young person marriage and parenting advice today, I would tell them they have to start teaching their partners to be helpful around the house right from the start because that job is forever. We cannot retire from housework and if both spouses have some knowledge of taking care of the household, then they can help each other during the retirement years. This makes family life more harmonious. I would also tell them to teach the children how to do household chores starting from a young age. It is not only important to learn academics, but both girls and boys need basic cleaning and sewing skills in life as well. I would also advise young people to think ahead about life, and do the little things now that will make a difference later. Don't binge, and I'm not just talking about food and exercise, although those things are important. But I'm also talking about money. If you make a lot of money, you can't just spend it all. No matter how much money you make, you have to go slowly and not do too many things at once.

Like the Confucius philosophy, *The Doctrine of the Mean*, that I learned all those years ago in school: As you go through life, you must always be aware that your actions have consequences. If a businessman spends all of his time working and neglects his family, there will be problems at home. This man is too far on one side of the road and his life is out of harmony. Likewise, a man who does not work is too far on the other side of the road and also out of harmony. But If you walk in the middle of the road, your life will be balanced, it will be calm and harmonious.

When I sit down and think back over everything, trying to analyze myself and understand why I am what I am, I realize that I have had an exceptional life. There have been four phases—the Japanese phase, the Chinese phase, the American phase, and the Mexican phase. Each of them has been important in my life and helped to make me the person that I am today. But the most influential on me was my Japanese education. I still admire the Japanese culture, and think it was a good education for me. The way they emphasized discipline, doing things just right, and physical education. I'm still like that.

That early Japanese training also taught me to be thrifty. Even after living in the U.S. all these years, where everything is in abundance, I am still thrifty. No matter how much money I have, I still take the bus. I could afford to take a limousine if I wanted to, but those kinds of things do not attract me. And when I hear news reports about things like a possible future water shortage, I take that seriously, and I do what I can. I do my part. Some people think it's too much work, but I think it is kind of fun. I don't think so much about luxuries, but I do think about function and about what works best. This is what attracts me and that came from my Japanese education.

To this day, I like figuring out how to do things better. For example, I save the rinse water from when I wash my face, collect it in a pail, and then use it to water the plants. I will also use the same pan to cook two or three different foods, before washing the pan. When I think about doing something or buying something, if it is not urgent, I usually don't do it or buy it right away. I just let it sit in my mind, or I write it down to remind myself. Sometimes I find out later that I did not have to do or buy that thing, or I think of some other way to take care of it, which ends up saving me time or money. These are just some of the things I do to simplify my life. I'm also very careful about using two different cutting boards to slice fruits and vegetables. I use one board to make the outer cuts, and then use another to cut the inside, the part we eat, all to minimize the risk of spreading bacteria which causes illness. It doesn't sound so significant, but maybe that's why I never get sick.

Most people do not think small things are worth the time. But they are simple to do, and for me, these little things—saving water, saving energy, taking an extra step to guard against bacteria—I think are my duty, and they help me to live my life in the middle of the road, and so it's good.

When I was a little girl, all I dreamed about was one day going to college and getting an education like my mother. I wasn't really interested in math or science; I wanted to learn how to cook, how to sew, and how to take care of the household. I guess I am just a homebody in that sense. When I left home at the age of 19 to come to the U.S., I had never done any of that for myself. We always had a housekeeper to cook our food and do the laundry, and then my mother did everything else for us. But as soon as I left for college, I had to learn to do all of that on my own. I even majored in home economics. That dream I had as a little girl came true, and that is what gave me the confidence to dream even more, to try even more, and to have such an exceptional life.

Sometime around the year 2000, I was lying down on the floor, just resting and listening to the radio, when I heard an opera singer performing an aria. He had such an incredible voice that I had to sit up and listen to the end. Up until that moment, I had never been interested in opera at all, but I suddenly had to know whom that voice belonged to.

I discovered the singer's name was Luciano Pavarotti, an Italian tenor, and that he regularly performed at the Metropolitan Opera House in New York. Joe and I decided to go see him perform live at the Met. Pavarotti had been performing for many years already, but after that we became members and went back to see his performance every season. Every year, as soon as we received The Met's opera schedule, I booked flights to New York and made reservations so that we could attend every single performance of his. I even got to meet him once, get his autograph, and have my picture taken with him inside a New York City record shop. Later, whenever he was performing in different parts of the world, we also made a point to travel there and see him perform whenever we could. We even visited his hometown, Modena, Italy.

Luciano Pavarotti opened my eyes and ears to the opera, and he paved the way for me to appreciate other opera singers and the style of music itself. But, to this day, I still think he was the best tenor singer.

Italian tenor Luciano Pavarroti signing his autograph for me.

One of my friends asked me why I think Pavarotti was so great, and my answer is that he had such a clear timbre. Whenever he sang, from the high timbre all the way down to the low timbre and back up again, he maintained the same voice, the same power, the same beauty with no change at all.

After the Seattle Opera House started offering better presentations (with the help of generous donations and under the management of Speight Jenkins), we decided to become members there, too. We have enjoyed many wonderful performances in our hometown of Seattle for many years. We still donate money to both the Metropolitan Opera House in New York and the Seattle Opera House.

As I have gotten older, I have grown to enjoy classic country music, and more recently I've started watching old country music performances from the '50s and '60s on YouTube. My favorite singers are Merle Haggard, Johnny Cash, Marty Robbins, Jim Reeves, Kris Kristofferson, and Waylon Jennings. I also like to read biographies about the singers because it helps me to better understand why so many of them wrote the music they did, how the lyrics so often are describing their own life's experiences, and why I find them so relatable. I turn to these old songs, these old lyrics to help me cope with the challenges of getting older and family situations, or sometimes just to help me forget for a little while.

One of my favorites is a song called "Storms Never Last" by Jessie Colter and Waylon Jennings. It is about a difficult situation that a couple is going through, but these words have brought me comfort during challenges of all kinds:

> I have followed you down so many roads baby
> I picked wild flowers and sung you soft sad songs
> And every road we took God knows our search was for the truth
> And the storm brewing now won't be the last.
>
> Storms never last do they baby
> Bad times all pass with the winds
> Your hand in mine stills the thunder
> And you make the sun want to shine.

POSTSCRIPT

The Chinese pronunciation of my name is Ting Chwen Erl 丁淳兒. The Japanese pronunciation is Tei Jun Ji. For both Chinese and Japanese names, the family name (surname) is written first, so Ting (丁) is my family name, then my first name, Chwen Erl (淳兒), comes after.

I am Chinese so I am known as Ting Chwen Erl, but in Japan I am known as Tei Jun Ji.

The Chinese name Ting is sometimes written phonetically as Dien or Ding.

"Ding is one of the simplest written Chinese family names written in two strokes. Although some do not practice Islam, the Ding clan remains as one of the better-known Hui clans around Quanzhou, Fujian that still identify as Muslim. These Hui clans merely require descent from Arab, Persian, or other Muslim forebears, and they need not be Muslim.

Other Romanizations include Ting, used in Taiwan, Hong Kong, and the Philippines."

– From Wikipedia

Maybe that is the reason the family name "Ting" is rare among the Chinese.

My siblings and I were all given our first names when we were born during the Japanese occupation of Taiwan, so we all have the naming characters of first names that are seen more in Japanese names. Quite often, the usage and meaning of the same character in Chinese and Japanese are somewhat different.

Mother told me naming children was a very important matter in China and Japan as the name will have an impact on the children as they grow up, so she consulted with my grandfather, her father, when deciding my name.

The first character of my first name "淳" (Chwen) in Chinese means pure, simple, honest. In Japanese it means kind to humanity, undecorated, or obedient. The second character "兒" (Erl) both in Chinese and Japanese means child. So "淳兒" means Obedient Child in Japanese. I've had many good laughs throughout my life at the irony of my mother naming me Obedient Child, since, as it turns out, I have often been anything *but*.

www.ingramcontent.com/pod-product-compliance
Lightning Source LLC
Chambersburg PA
CBHW041307240426
43661CB00037B/1462/J